CHRIST
at the Center of
PASTORAL MINISTRY

CHRIST
at the Center of
PASTORAL MINISTRY

The Difference Jesus Makes in Pastoral Theology, Spiritual Leadership, and Ministry Practices

RICHARD THOMAS VANN JR.

Christ at the Center of Pastoral Ministry:
The Difference Jesus Makes in Pastoral Theology, Spiritual Leadership,
and Ministry Practices

Copyright © 2022 Richard Thomas Vann Jr.

All Rights Reserved

ISBN 978-1-955295-21-5

Unless otherwise noted, all Scripture is taken from the New King James Version®. Copyright © 1982 by Thomas Nelson. Used by permission. All rights reserved.

Scripture quotations marked NASB® are taken from the New American Standard Bible®, Copyright © 1995 by The Lockman Foundation. Used by permission. All rights reserved. www.lockman.org.

Scripture quotations marked NIV are taken from the Holy Bible, New International Version®, NIV®. Copyright © 1973, 1978, 1984, 2011 by Biblica, Inc.™ Used by permission of Zondervan. All rights reserved worldwide. www.zondervan.com The "NIV" and "New International Version" are trademarks registered in the United States Patent and Trademark Office by Biblica, Inc.™

Scripture quotations marked HCSB are taken from the Holman Christian Standard Bible®, Copyright © 1999, 2000, 2002, 2003, 2009 by Holman Bible Publishers. Used by permission. Holman Christian Standard Bible®, Holman CSB®, and HCSB® are federally registered trademarks of Holman Bible Publishers.

Scripture quotations marked KJV are taken from the Holy Bible, King James Version. Public domain.

Courier Publishing
100 Manly Street
Greenville, South Carolina 29601
CourierPublishing.com

PUBLISHED IN THE UNITED STATES OF AMERICA

Dedication

This book is dedicated to the pastors who influenced me for Jesus Christ, beginning with my father's pastor from his childhood and mine, Rev. J.M. Duncan, who baptized him in 1929 and lived next door to us when I was growing up. I played behind Preacher Duncan's big study built behind their house, and as a child I always wondered what he was doing when he went in there.

The churches and chapels I have served as pastor and chaplain deserve my deepest thanks for calling and permitting me to serve Christ with them in those communities in Virginia, Turkey, Colorado, South Carolina, Greece, Georgia, Wisconsin, New Jersey, and Texas.

Next, I want to dedicate this book to the theological students I have taught about pastoral and chaplaincy ministry at Southwestern Baptist Theological Seminary and Dallas Baptist University. Many of these former students are serving as pastors and staff ministers of churches and chaplains in the Army, Navy, Air Force, hospitals, prisons, detention centers, airports, and the corporate world. I had the special privilege of teaching our fourth son in seminary who served as a pastor, now an Army chaplain, and my son-in-law, a missionary-pastor in the Dominican Republic. All six of our children and their spouses have been a tremendous source of love and encouragement to me through the years of pastoral and chaplaincy ministry.

Lastly, and most importantly, I must dedicate this book to the woman from California I met one Wednesday night at a prayer meeting in District Heights, Maryland and married four months later in her home church in Rancho Cordova, California. Marta has been my constant companion in ministry to this day — from my calling to serve Christ as a chaplain assistant, pastor, associate pastor, church staff minister, military chaplain, and professor of Christian ministry in a college, seminary extension center in Greece, theological seminary, and graduate school of ministry.

Table of Contents

Foreword		ix
Endorsements		xi
Tribute		xv
Introduction		xvii
Chapter 1	The Shepherding Pastor	3
Chapter 2	The Good Shepherd	13
Chapter 3	Gifted Christians in Ministry	25
Chapter 4	Chosen to Serve Jesus in Gospel Ministry	39
Chapter 5	Jesus and the Ordinances	49
Chapter 6	Infant and Child Dedications, Weddings, and Funerals	63
Chapter 7	The Pastor's Prayer and Home Life	75
Chapter 8	Jesus and Shepherding Care	85
Chapter 9	Counseling Like Jesus	97
Chapter 10	Conducting Church Ministry Business	109
Chapter 11	Worship, Preaching, Evangelism, Missions, Church Planting	123
Chapter 12	Spiritual and Administrative Leadership	135
Chapter 13	Team Ministry and Discipleship Training	153
Chapter 14	Pastoral Ethics, Etiquette, Politics, Legal Issues, Church Discipline	163
Chapter 15	Bloom Where You Are Planted	181
Chapter 16	Reviewing the Basics of a Pastor Serving Christ in a New Testament Church	191
About the Author		207

Foreword

Tom Vann earned my respect as a Christian, a pastor, and a leader the day I met him. I began my first full-time pastorate in an established church at the age of twenty-four. At forty-one years of age, I resigned that ministry to accept the invitation to teach ministry students at nearby Criswell College. The church organized a search committee and called a military chaplain who had recently relocated to the metroplex from a different state as their interim pastor. I raised an eyebrow, but did not interfere. I met him after the fact, and was immediately confident not only that they had made the right choice, but that God had led them to a shepherd who would guide them selflessly, wisely, and spiritually through the transition to come. Because I had a Master of Divinity, a Ph.D. in Humanities, and more than seventeen years of pastoral experience leading a church I loved and that loved me, I thought I knew something. Just a few minutes with Tom — with the surprising juxtaposition of crew cut and jovial gentility, of military propriety and kind patience, of practical experience and genuine spirituality — and what I knew was that he knew a lot more than I did, and that my former church was in the best possible hands. In fact, I remember saying to myself, only half joking, that they might feel like this interim was their first real pastor in a long time.

There are many ways to influence people. I do it in a classroom, as a college president, as pulpit supply, with occasional writings, and with a broadcast turned podcast. But I know of no one else who can influence people's lives long-term more than a pastor. Week in and week out, pastors shape how their flocks understand, prioritize, and respond to the world around them. They exhort and teach, certainly.

But in delivery rooms and funeral parlors, at wedding rehearsals and counseling sessions, pastors shape and guide, encourage and comfort their people. Because that influence is so significant, it is critical that pastors grasp the theological basis of their office and the nature of spiritual leadership, as well as the practical and technical skills required to fulfill such a high calling.

In this work, Tom Vann provides from his decades of study, practice, and leadership exactly what every person committed to serving as Christian shepherd ought to understand. The fact that he does so by focusing on the ministry and teaching of Jesus is not a surprise. His own spirit testifies that he practices what he preaches and what he has written. Looking back on my time in pastoral leadership roles, I know that I and the people I served would have benefited had I known Tom Vann and had his guidance from the beginning. I pray current pastors and those preparing for the role will receive exactly that help in the pages of this book.

Finally, I hope and pray that what the Spirit has produced in Tom Vann — so evident in his kindness, encouragement, and peacemaking — will be multiplied in every person he influences through this work.

Dr. Barry Creamer
President, Criswell College
Dallas, Texas

Endorsements

Dr. Tom Vann is the epitome and embodiment of pastoral ministry. I met Dr. Vann in the fall of 2004 at Southwestern Baptist Theological Seminary and he was my professor for two pastoral ministry courses. They were refreshing, to say the least — because he did not just teach about pastoral ministry, he ministered and shepherded his students. Dr. Vann was everyone's favorite professor. From the moment I stepped into his classroom, I began to learn what grace and mercy were all about.

Since that point, we have stayed in contact, and he has been supportive to my family and me for the past several years. When I pastored in Van Alstyne, Texas, he came and preached a revival at the church I was serving. When I moved to South Carolina, he succeeded me in ministry as the pastor of the Villas at Bear Creek Fellowship, where he is still serving. Most recently, he recommended me for a pastoral position at Pinecrest Baptist Church in Charleston, South Carolina, where I just recently began serving. I cannot think of a more fitting person to learn pastoral ministry from than Dr. Vann, because I feel like he taught me everything I know. When one picks up his book to read it, they can do so with an assurance that it is not just words on a page, it is the story of his life.

Rev. Billy Stockton
Pastor, Pinecrest Baptist Church
Charleston, South Carolina

I have personally benefited from Dr. Vann in the seminary classroom! Through *Christ at the Center of Pastoral Ministry: The Difference Jesus Makes in Pastoral Theology, Spiritual Leadership, and Ministry Practices*, Dr. Vann invites all of us into the classroom of ministry from a wise and experienced man of God. You won't regret taking the time to read this book!

Dr. Nick Floyd
Senior Pastor
Cross Church Northwest Arkansas
Springdale, Arkansas

What a wonderful book! Dr. Tom Vann has provided a resource that should be in the library of every pastor and should be required reading at every seminary. Not only that, but every Christian would be blessed to read this book as well.

Rev. Jim Tucker
Senior Pastor
Deer Park First Baptist Church
Deer Park, Texas

Tom Vann's classes were some of the most valuable (and intensely practical!) of my seminary years. Reading this book let me learn all over again the art of pastoral ministry from a seasoned shepherd. That was a spacious place to return to after nearly twenty years and countless complex pastoral situations later. It was a gift to be reminded of how much of my practical ministry was informed by Dr. Vann's faithfulness and teaching. I think yours will be as well.

Dr. Jared Musgrove
Executive Pastor for Spiritual Formation & Groups
The WELL Community Church
Argyle, Texas

Dr. Vann calls us to a return of the pastor as shepherd. His work is biblically grounded, practically applied, and thorough in its implications for pastoral ministry. His pastoral heart is felt in this work with the kind of insight and perspective that is helpful to every called minister to follow in the steps of Jesus. Read and let your soul be stirred for ministry again!

Dr. Phillip Dunn
Senior Pastor
First Baptist Church, Mount Juliet
Mount Juliet, Tennessee

Written with the wisdom of a pastor, the heart of an evangelist, and the intellect of an academician, Dr. Vann has woven together in this volume the multifaceted nature of ministry and pointed us toward ministry's theological end: Christ. This work is a culmination of a lifetime of Dr. Vann's ministry where he has consistently pointed his church, his students, his soldiers, and the lost to Christ. No one has demonstrated better a love for Christ and people than Dr. Vann. Drink from this well that is filled with wisdom, Scripture, and experience from one who has shown us "The Difference Jesus Makes."

Dr. Lewis Richerson
Lead Pastor
Woodlawn Baptist Church
Baton Rouge, Louisianas

Tribute

After researching and the painstaking writing of dissertations for doctorates at the University of South Carolina and Midwestern Baptist Theological Seminary, this is my first book. I am so grateful for the careful editing and recommendations from Butch Blume and the staff of Courier Publishing, Greenville, South Carolina.

After considering a number of publishers, I decided on Courier Publishing for several reasons. First, my mother's people are all South Carolinians. She was raised in Williamston where Butch Blume and his family live. My mother's parents and siblings lived with her grandparents for years in a big white house where Calvary Baptist Church of Williamston is located today. Butch knows where my grandparents and other kin are buried. My grandmother later moved to Greenville to live with my aunt after my grandfather died, and I always looked forward to trips to Greenville through the years.

Secondly, for eighteen years (1982-2000) I researched the life, pastoral and higher educational ministry of Jonathan Maxcy, the first president of the South Carolina College (1804-20). My study in the archives of the South Caroliniana Library thrilled me, as I learned about this godly Christian minister and educator, who preached to the Baptists when he first came to town. While working on doctoral studies in South Carolina, in addition to a pastorate, from 1988-92 I served as a grant administrator and faculty member at Williamsburg Technical College, Kingstree.

Thirdly, I served as an Army chaplain at Fort Jackson (1982-85) and was a member of First Baptist Church, Columbia, South Carolina during those years. Dr. Marshall Edwards was a wonderful pastor and

Dr. Philip Steyne served as a fine interim pastor to the congregation prior to Dr. Wendell Estep being called as pastor in 1986. After a two-year Army chaplaincy assignment in Greece, our family moved back to South Carolina, where I became the pastor of Bethel Baptist Church, Olanta, from 1987-93. It was a rich blessing to serve the Lord in a rural community and church like I knew growing up in Murfreesboro, North Carolina, at Meherrin Baptist Church (1729), the state's second-oldest existing Baptist church.

Let me commend and recommend Courier Publishing for any pastor, Christian, or church with a story to tell about the Christian life and the work of Jesus Christ in the world.

Introduction

Pastors and gospel ministers through the centuries have benefited from what the prophets and apostles penned in the Old and New Testaments and what pastoral theologians and pastors have taught and written that has been preserved. This book will look to Jesus, the author and finisher of our faith (Heb. 12:2), and to the Holy Scriptures (2 Tim. 3:14-17) for a Christ-centered approach to pastoral theology, spiritual leadership, and ministry practices.

Despite growing up in a Bible-believing church from cradle roll, I did not surrender to the lordship of Jesus Christ until I was twenty-one years of age after reading the New Testament in a modern translation and watching Billy Graham preach a message on the Prodigal Son televised from the 1969 Madison Square Garden Crusade. My life changed dramatically that night, and I have endeavored to conduct a Christ-centered approach to life and ministry ever since. Shortly after my commitment to Christ, I began serving the Lord as an Air Force chapel services specialist and a mission chapel pastor later in 1971. I am eternally grateful, after more than fifty years of ministry, to be serving as a professor of Christian ministry at a Christ-honoring university and as the pastor of an interdenominational Christian fellowship of senior adults. My wife, a hospital chaplain, and I are members of a Baptist church, and she has been at my side in life and ministry ever since we married in 1970.

The idea for the title of the book came from a professor I had in a doctor of ministry seminar and from a university graduate course I teach. My DMin dissertation is entitled "The Difference Jesus Makes: A Return to Biblically Based Pastoral Theology, Ministry, and Leadership for Pastors and Chaplains." In my years of ministry, I have served as an Air Force chaplain assistant, pastor, Army chaplain, and professor at a Christian college, seminary, and university. I am blessed beyond measure how God is using students who have studied with me since I first began teaching individuals preparing for Christian ministry in 1975.

While I am committed to the Protestant canon of Scripture (sixty-six books), I have found myself absorbed by the life and teachings of Jesus. My favorite way of reading about Jesus is from my well-worn Harmonies of the Gospels. My first chronological study of Jesus' life and teachings was A.T. Robertson's *A Harmony of the Gospels for Students of the Life of Christ*. Next, I transitioned to *A Harmony of the Words and Works of Jesus Christ* by J. Dwight Pentecost. I currently read *The New NASB Harmony of the Gospels* by Robert L. Thomas and Stanley N. Gundry. Since 2010 when I teach a course on the Gospels, I require the reading of a harmony.

The life, teaching, extended ministry, death and resurrection of Jesus, and empowerment by the Holy Spirit from the days of Pentecost ten days after His ascension have flooded my soul in pastoral theology, spiritual leadership, and ministry practices since 1969. I am deeply indebted to some godly pastors who influenced and mentored me in my earliest years of pastoral ministry, all of whom are with the Lord now.

I am grateful to have taken a pastoral ministry class with Leith Anderson, an adjunct professor at Denver Seminary who at the time was serving as pastor of Calvary Church, Longmont. He went on to become the pastor of Wooddale Church in Minneapolis for thirty-five years and then president of the National Association of Evangelicals from 2002-2003 and 2006-2019. Donald Burdick, my major New Testament professor at Denver Seminary and a former pastor, greatly impacted my love for and understanding of the New Testament Scriptures.

In addition to some pastoral mentors whom God provided to guide me, I am grateful for learning about *The Didache, The Teaching of the Lord to the Gentiles by the Twelve Apostles*, the earliest extant training guide for the church probably written in the second century. Some early church fathers considered it Scripture, but it did not make it into the canon. I keep a copy of it in my Bible and read it from time to time as inspirational literature. I have distributed copies of an English translation of *The Didache* to my ministry students. The first part deals with the Two Ways (the way of life versus the way of death); the second part consists of instructions regarding food, baptism, fasting, prayer, the eucharist, liturgical prayers, and assorted practical issues related to various ministries and positions of leadership.[1]

In preparation for my dissertation on pastoral theology, I consulted many writings and books by pastors and theologians from the second century until today. Among those men of God beyond Scripture writers whose writings have deeply influenced me most in ministry are the following: Clement of Rome, Ignatius of Antioch, Polycarp, Eusebius, Gregory the Great, Martin Bucer, Richard Baxter, Charles Finney, Charles Spurgeon, Charles Jefferson, W.A. Criswell, Carl Volz, Thomas Oden, James Bryant, Billy Graham, Henry Blackaby, Oswald Sanders, Warren Wiersbe, Andrew Purves, Stephen Olford, Jerry Falwell, John Bisagno, Erwin Lutzer, Bob Russell, and John MacArthur. Each of these men have put me on high ground in thinking about pastoral theology, spiritual leadership, and ministry practices. It has been a blessing to draw from the well of these godly men.

---

1 Michael W. Holmes, translator and editor, *The Apostolic Fathers in English*, third edition (Grand Rapids: Baker Academic, 1989, 2006), 163-71.

CHRIST

at the Center of

PASTORAL MINISTRY

CHAPTER 1

THE SHEPHERDING PASTOR

The Apostle Peter wrote the elders of churches in Pontus, Galatia, Cappadocia, Asia, and Bithynia to "shepherd the flock of God which is among you, serving as overseers, not by compulsion but willingly, not for dishonest gain but eagerly; nor as being lords over those entrusted to you, but being examples to the flock; and when the Chief Shepherd appears, you will receive the crown of glory that does not fade away" (1 Pet. 5:2-4).

In speaking of shepherding the flock, Peter was using a metaphor Jesus had employed in His earthly ministry (John 10:1-18; Luke 15:3-7), and it must have been firmly etched in his mind especially after the resurrected Christ spoke to him about feeding the sheep of His flock (John 21:15-17). Peter and those elders have long since passed off the scene, but God is still calling out pastors to shepherd the flock in His churches. It is a high honor to be called by Jesus to shepherd His flock, and when He returns, He will reward those who have served faithfully as pastors under Him.

Having followed Jesus for several years, Peter knew the character and conduct required of pastors, how they are to serve willingly and not under compulsion, eagerly and not for financial gain, leading by example and never lording over those entrusted for ministry. What a high calling pastors receive from the Lord! As a first-year seminary student, I attended Dr. W.A. Criswell's School of the Prophets at the

First Baptist Church of Dallas. I remember him saying to us who had gathered there from all over the country: "The highest calling in the world is not to be a prince, a pope, a potentate, or a president, but to be a pastor." When I asked him a ministry question from the seating area, he replied to me, "Young man, preach the Word and be a sweet and loving Christian." I have never forgotten those words which became the center of my ministry as a pastor, military chaplain, and professor.

Shortly after graduation from Baylor University in 1897, Criswell's predecessor George W. Truett, having raised money from 1891-93 to rescue Baylor from a large indebtedness, was unanimously elected to become the president of Baylor. After prayer and deep reflection, Truett responded, "I have sought and found the shepherd's heart and I cannot come." For him, the call to be a shepherd of God's people took priority over the call to be an educational administrator. Truett had served as the pastor of East Waco Baptist Church (1893-97) and went on to serve as pastor of First Baptist Church, Dallas (1897-1944) until his death.

Four characteristics appear to sum up the pastoral ministry of Dr. George W. Truett:

Humility — honors never puffed him up

Simplicity — his messages though profound were always simple, filled with illustrations to explain the Christian life

Spirituality — people felt like they were in the presence of the Lord when with him

Preaching — his sermons were conversational and his voice filled with pathos would make his congregation weep and never be ashamed of it.

Truett served as a model of a good shepherd to the followers of Christ and those who needed to come to know Him.[1]

---

1 "George W. Truett, 1867-1944, Baptist Pastor," https://believersweb.org/george-w-truett-1867-1944-baptist-pastor, accessed January 13, 2022.

Introduction to Biblical Pastoral Theology

Theological education for pastoral ministry throughout the twentieth century, and continuing in the twenty-first century, has become increasingly pragmatic and practical, moving further and further away from its biblically based moorings. Derek Tidball articulates this proposition succinctly: "For most of this century [speaking of the twentieth century] pastoral theology has been in the doldrums. At the start of the century, it had largely degenerated from being a serious theological discipline to not much more than handy tips on 'how to' practice ministry."[2]

Deviations from the biblical pattern for pastoral theology crept into the church in the second century and continued through the medieval period of the church. From the days of the Protestant Reformation, the course to teach seminarians the study of the office and functions of the pastor-shepherd began to be called "poimenics"[3] or "pastoral theology." Thomas Oden in his classic text on pastoral theology bemoans the fact that "the deliberate study of the pastoral office and its functions has been neglected in our time."[4]

No area of pastoral theology has been more impacted than pastoral care. Andrew Purves observes that "biblical and theological perspectives ... no longer shape the practice of much pastoral work. The modern pastoral care movement within the North American Protestant theological academy by and large revolves around psychological categories regarding human experience and symbolic interpretations

---

2 Derek Tidball, *Skillful Shepherds: Explorations in Pastoral Theology* (Leicester: Apollos, 1997), 13.
3 "Poimenics" is a term from the Greek word ποιμήν [poimēn] meaning "shepherd."
4 Thomas C. Oden, *Pastoral Theology: Essentials of Ministry* (San Francisco: HarperSanFrancisco, 1989), viii.

about God."⁵ Purves suggests that "a relatively comfortable synthesis results in which pastoral theology, and consequently, pastoral practice in the church, have become concerned largely with questions of meaning rather than truth, acceptable functioning rather than discipleship, and a concern for self-actualization and self-realization rather than salvation."⁶

David Fisher, in an address to the Evangelical Theological Society in 2010 entitled "Whatever Happened to Pastoral Theology?", tied the beginning of this drift to Washington Gladden's book *The Christian Pastor*, published in 1898, and his 1902 Beecher Lectures at Yale, on Social Salvation.⁷ Fisher believes that Gladden's writing, greatly influenced by the social sciences, led to the death of the discipline of pastoral theology. Thereafter, pastoral theology became entirely functional in pastoral ministry courses for seminarians that dealt primarily with the practical aspects of the ministry, including such teaching as he experienced on proper lighting in a church parking lot.⁸

Glenn Wagner says, "It is difficult to find a seminary track in pastoral theology that is solidly rooted in the Scriptures. Most seminaries now teach 'practical ministry,' a set of learned skills rooted in psychological and sociological principles. This approach isn't theological in the true sense of the terms, for practical ministry is a philosophical and programmatic approach to conducting ministry."⁹ Wagner states his case regarding the demise of pastoral theology in America: "The problem? Like Esau, we pastors have sold our biblical

---

5 Andrew Purves, *Pastoral Theology in the Classical Tradition* (Louisville: Westminster John Knox Press, 2001), 3.
6 Ibid.
7 David Fisher, "Whatever Happened to Pastoral Theology?" Address to the Evangelical Theological Society, 17 November 2010 (Atlanta, Georgia), 4.
8 Fisher, "Whatever Happened to Pastoral Theology?" 5.
9 E. Glenn Wagner, *Escape From Church, Inc.: The Return of the Pastor-Shepherd* (Grand Rapids: Zondervan, 1999), 57.

birthright as shepherds called by God for the pottage of skills and gimmicks designed by humans. We have misunderstood the role of the pastor and defined it incorrectly. We have left our biblical and theological moorings."[10] Wagner speaks to the consequences: "The result? Our churches are struggling mightily, Christians are wandering from the faith, and pastors are burning out at alarming rates."[11]

This book seeks to return students to a pastoral theology and ministry practices based upon the teachings of Scripture and insights from pastoral leaders down through the history of the church who practiced Bible-based, Christ-honoring, and Spirit-filled pastoral ministry.

The Pastoral Office and Identity

The New Testament reveals that after the sending out of the apostles to the ends of the earth to preach the gospel and make disciples (Matt. 28:19-20), the leadership in the churches became invested in men called bishops, elders, pastors. These terms were used interchangeably to describe the primary spiritual leaders of the churches. Scripture identifies the shepherding office as that of a *bishop* (Phil. 1:1; 1 Tim. 3:1-2; Tit. 1:7), *elder* (Tit. 1:5), and *pastor* (Eph. 4:11). All three descriptors of church shepherding leadership may be seen in Acts 20:17, 28: "From Miletus, he [Paul] sent to Ephesus and called for the *elders* of the church. ... Therefore, take heed to yourselves and to all the flock, among which the Holy Spirit has made you *overseers*, to *shepherd (pastor)* the church of God which He purchased with His own blood." These spiritual leaders of the church were preceded by and assisted by Spirit-filled men (Acts 6:3-6), prophets and teachers (Acts 13:1-2), then deacons (Phil. 1:1, 1 Tim. 3:8-13) and men and women in the churches (Rom. 16:1-16).

---

10 Wagner, *Escape From Church*, 17.
11 Ibid.

The title of *overseer* or *bishop* (*episkopos*) likely emerged in Gentile congregations. Overseers (bishops) were administrators in social institutions such as burial associations, athletic clubs, and other special interest groups, including municipal governments. The term began to be applied in churches for senior leaders who would superintend and give administrative oversight to the mission and ministry of the church. While the term may have been borrowed from the culture, the church gave it spiritual meaning and authority. Qualifications for serving as a bishop are stated in 1 Timothy 3:1-7 and Titus 1:5-9.

The term *elder* (*presbyter*) was undoubtedly borrowed from Judaism, as each synagogue had its group of elders which functioned as a court and governing body. An elder was a mature man in spiritual leadership. Early churches appear to have had a plurality of elders, with a ruling elder who came to be called a bishop. Elders (*presbyteroi*) appear for the first time in the New Testament in association with the collection for famine relief among the Jewish Christians of Jerusalem (Acts 11:30). They administered the relief sent by the disciples of the church at Antioch. Paul and Barnabas appointed elders in every church they planted in Derbe, Lystra, Iconium, and Antioch of Pisidia (Acts 14:23). The elders of the Jerusalem church are described meeting with the apostles at the Council of Jerusalem to settle the issue of Gentiles turning in faith to Christ (Acts 15). Qualifications for elders are stated in Titus 1:5-9.

The term for the office of *pastor* (*shepherd*) is used only once in the New Testament (Eph. 4:11) in the plural as pastors (*poimenas*). A shepherd would lead, protect, and guide a flock of sheep, and the parallel applies to a pastor of a church. This term describes the gift, role, responsibilities, and duties of the church leader. Earlier you read how Peter exhorted the elders of the churches to shepherd (pastor) the flock of God (1 Pet. 5:2) and he shares how this must be done (1 Pet. 5:2-3). This ministry must be carried out under Christ the Chief Shepherd (1 Pet. 5:4).

Calling to the Pastorate

The ministry of serving Christ as a pastor (under-shepherd) is not a job. It is a vocation, the answering of a specific call or invitation from the Lord and His people to lead a church. A calling to Christian leadership and ministry is "the unmistakable conviction an individual possesses that God wants him to do a specific task ... God calls men to shepherd God's flock and to care for its well-being, to show God's people by example and instruction how they should live lives worthy of God their savior."[12] Calling is an inward conviction based upon the Word of God and the Holy Spirit that one should serve in spiritual leadership, and it will be confirmed by the church.

James M. George has well written, "The call of God to vocational ministry is different from God's call to salvation and his call to service issued to all Christians. It is a call to selected men to serve as leaders in the church. To serve in such leadership capacities, recipients of this call must have assurance that God has so selected them."[13] George lists five criteria[14] leading to an assurance of the calling to serve in vocational ministry as a pastor:

1. *Confirmation of the Call by Others* — A church recognizes one's calling and sets a man apart to serve in a particular place of ministry as a pastor or leader in ministry (Acts 16:1-2; 1 Tim. 4:14; Tit. 1:5).
2. *Confirmation from God* — God opens a door for pastoral, missionary, or church-planting ministry (1 Cor. 16:8-9).

---

12 Derek Prime and Alistair Begg, *On Being a Pastor: Understanding Our Calling and Work* (Chicago: Moody, 2004), 18.
13 James M. George, "The Call to Pastoral Ministry," in *Pastoral Ministry: How to Shepherd Biblically* (Nashville: Thomas Nelson, 2005), 81.
14 Ibid., 84-91.

3. *Possession of Abilities Necessary to Serve in Leadership Capacities* — Christ has given spiritual leadership gifts to the church (Eph. 4:11-13). The ability to shepherd with oversight as an example to God's people is key and essential (Acts 20:28; 1 Pet. 5:2, 3). An essential component in the calling is that the candidate should be "able to teach" (1 Tim. 3:2).
4. *A Longing to Serve as a Pastor* — The one called has a desire for the office (1 Tim. 3:1). The 1 Timothy 3:1 text reveals, "If any man aspires (*oregetai*) to the office of overseer, it is a fine work he desires (*epithumei*) to do" (NASB). The first Greek word means "to stretch out toward, to reach out for, to yearn for"; the second word means "to long for, passionately desire"; the desire would be for the office in the sense of serving in the office but not for the status of the office.
5. *Moral Integrity* — A lifestyle of godly spiritual and moral integrity (1 Tim. 3:2-7, 4:16; 2 Tim. 2:19; Tit. 1:5-9; 1 Pet. 1:15-16). Pastors need to be more concerned about their integrity and godliness than their abilities and giftedness. Sadly, gifted individuals have brought reproach to Christ and His church by their lack of moral integrity.

Pastoral Functions

To move this chapter forward, here is a basic list of pastoral functions church leaders must be prepared to perform in ministry. Many more insights will be explained in the chapters that will follow. These tasks will be reviewed in the last chapter as they must be imbedded indelibly in the mind and heart of the pastor.

- **Leader in worship** — providing worship services that draw people into the presence of God.

- **Model of the Christian life** — being an example of a Christ-centered person in one's personal life and home.
- **Preaching** — proclaiming the Word of God accurately and powerfully.
- **Teaching** — studying, exegeting, and explaining the Word of God.
- **Praying** — maintaining a disciplined life of prayer.
- **Pastoral care and counseling** — visiting, attending to the life issues, and listening to parishioners share their burdens and blessings.
- **Leadership and administration** — planning, organizing, programming, staffing, implementing, and evaluating ministries and programs.
- **Promoter of evangelism** — leading the church in evangelism to win people to faith in Christ.
- **Dispensing benevolence** — providing for the needy in the church and community as resources are available.
- **Adjudicating disputes** — seeking to resolve conflicts among members of the church.
- **Church discipline** — admonishing and correcting church members needing to repent, confess sin, be forgiven, and to forgive.[15]

---

[15] I am thankful for insight into this list, which I expanded, from Carl A. Volz's *Pastoral Life and Practice in the Early Church* (Minneapolis: Augsburg Fortress, 1990), 47. His informative book considers pastoral theology, leadership, and ministry practices from the first to the fifth century.

CHAPTER 2

THE GOOD SHEPHERD

In John 10:11-16 and 27-30, we read about Jesus the Good Shepherd. This teaching from the Apostle John rings in our hearts and souls because of such passages in the Old Testament as Psalm 23, where David wrote, "The Lord is my shepherd." Most of us growing up in small towns, cities, and suburbs know very little about raising sheep, but the thought of a good shepherd leading, guiding, providing, protecting, loving, healing, and rescuing sheep relates to us as God's sheep in churches wanting a good pastor-shepherd.

For those who are given the privilege of serving as pastor-shepherds (under-shepherds) to God's sheep in the church, there are some wonderful truths in John 10 that can be applied to the work of a pastor in this passage:

(1) The Good Shepherd gives His life for the sheep (vv. 11, 15). No sacrifice is too great for good shepherds. It took Jesus all the way to the cross, and we who serve as pastors must die to self each day as we minister on behalf of Christ.

(2) The Good Shepherd is not a hireling (vv. 12-13). A hireling watches over the sheep only because he is paid to do so. The good shepherd watches after the sheep because he is responsible for the sheep and cares deeply for them. When danger comes, the good shepherd will not abandon the sheep or flee. Pastors must daily be on guard for the work of the devil and his minions in the work of ministry.

(3) The Good Shepherd knows His sheep and they know Him (vv. 3-4, 14). He knows those in his flock by name and their individual characteristics. We can best pray for our church members if we know them and have a relationship with them.

(4) The Good Shepherd will be followed because He knows God and points the sheep to eternal life (vv. 27-28). A good pastor will be listened to and learned from as he follows the Lord and points the congregation to eternal life in Christ.

(5) The Good Shepherd has many sheep in His flock beyond those in the individual fold (v. 16). A good pastor will minister to Christians beyond his own congregation as he has the opportunity without trying to steal sheep.

Ministry in the New Testament

In the earliest years of the first century following the death, burial, resurrection, and ascension of Jesus, the church did not have clergy as we understand that role today in terms of education, recognition, salary, or societal and political status. The early spiritual leaders of the church are referred to as apostles, prophets, teachers, evangelists, pastors and teachers for the work of ministry in "edifying the body of Christ till we all come to the unity of the faith and of the knowledge of the Son of God, to a perfect man, to the measure of the stature of the fullness of Christ" (Eph. 4:11-13).

The Twelve (including Matthias) and other apostles named in the New Testament (Paul, Barnabas, Apollos, Silvanus or Silas, Timothy, Epaphroditus, and James) were among the earliest spiritual leaders in the primitive church. The original twelve attempted to guide the church from Jerusalem until the Romans destroyed the city in AD 70. The apostles for the most part became missionaries even before the destruction of the temple. They went out to the known world to preach the gospel and make disciples. You can read their stories in John Foxe's *Book of Martyrs*, originally published in 1563.

Some of the spiritually gifted men in the church in time were called bishops and elders (Tit. 1:5-7). After prayer and fasting, Paul and Barnabas appointed elders for each of the churches they established and committed them to the Lord (Acts 14:23). Qualifications were laid down for this office in 1 Timothy 3:1-7 and Titus 1:5-9. We will consider these qualifications in a later chapter. Also, in the churches were individuals gifted by the Holy Spirit (1 Cor. 12:11) to serve as instruments of miracles, with gifts of healings, helps, administrations, and various kinds of tongues (1 Cor. 12:28).

After the church in Jerusalem came into existence, seven men were selected by the church to settle an issue regarding the distribution of food to the Jewish and Gentile widows. These were to be men of good reputation, full of the Holy Spirit, faith, and wisdom. This would allow the apostles to devote themselves to prayer and the ministry of the Word (Acts 7:1-6). After prayer, hands were laid on them by the apostles to set them apart for this ministry. The laying on of hands was simply confirmation of the selection to the position. Eventually, these ministers came to be known as "deacons" to assist the bishops/elders/pastors (Phil. 1:1; 1 Tim. 3:8-13).

How Spiritual Leaders Are Trained

The Apostle Paul, like Jesus, knew the importance of face-to-face, hands-on training of contemporaries in ministry and those who were to come after them in succeeding generations. Paul wrote Timothy in his Second Letter to commit the things he learned "to faithful men who will be able to teach others also" (2 Tim. 2:2). There is no better way of training pastors for gospel ministry than the way Jesus trained the Twelve. Robert Coleman's *The Master Plan of Evangelism* summarizes eight guiding principles Jesus used in preparing the disciples for ministry.[1] The principles our Lord used will aid the church in training pastors and gospel ministers.

Selection — After a night of prayer out on a mountain, Jesus chose, or called to Himself, twelve men from a larger group of disciples whom He named apostles (Luke 6:12-13). Women accompanied Jesus and the disciples on preaching missions, but their role appears to have been reserved for support of Jesus and the apostles (Luke 8:1-3).

Association — Jesus made a practice of being with those He called. This was the essence of His training program — just letting His disciples follow Him ... all Jesus did to teach these men His way was draw them close to Himself. He was His own school and curriculum. Jesus chose these twelve men that "they might be with Him" (Mark 3:14). He walked the roads of Palestine, rode in boats, ate, and slept with His disciples, using the teachable moments of the day and evening to talk with them about the kingdom of God. At times He would speak to the multitudes, then in private answer the questions of the disciples and explain what He meant (Matt. 13:36).

Consecration — Jesus expected the apostles to obey Him by keeping His commandments centered in love for Him (John 14:15, 23). Following Jesus would require consecration, in that the apostles would deny self and take up a cross daily (Matt. 16:24; Mark 8:34; Luke 9:23). To follow Jesus in discipleship meant self-denial, renouncing self-interest, the highest fulfillment of a human being, in view of taking up a cross, a known Roman symbol of gruesome suffering and death.

Impartation — In order to follow and obey Jesus, the disciples would need an impartation of what Jesus had received from His Heavenly

---

[1] Robert E. Coleman, *The Master Plan of Evangelism* (Grand Rapids: Fleming H. Revell, 1993), 27-106.

Father, namely His Word, His peace, His love, His joy, His power, and the opportunity to participate in His kingdom. They would need to receive an impartation of the Spirit of God (John 20:22) to empower them to fulfill the commission they had received (Matt. 28:19-20; Mark 16:15). Then they would need a subsequent mighty baptism of the Holy Spirit (Acts 1:4-5, 8) for empowerment to take the message of their Master to the ends of the earth, which they received at Pentecost ten days after Jesus ascended back to heaven (Acts 2:1-13).

Demonstration — Jesus not only taught concepts to the disciples, He demonstrated His teaching. For example, He taught them how to pray and gave them a model prayer (Matt. 6:13; Luke 11:2-4), and on occasion the disciples observed Him at prayer (Luke 9:18, 11:1) and heard Him praying (John 17:1-26). The disciples wanted more than an explanation; they wanted a demonstration. Time and again, Jesus modeled what He taught them about preaching, teaching, healing, deliverance, evangelism, and benevolent care.

Delegation — In training His disciples for ministry, Jesus understood the principle of delegation, which Moses learned from his father-in-law, Jethro (Ex. 18:13-27). Jesus knew the value of assigning ministry tasks to the disciples, including getting food and arranging accommodations for the group as they followed Him. He also let them baptize some people who were drawn to His message (John 4:2). Eventually He sent them out two by two on preaching missions (Matt. 10:5-15; Mark 6:7-13; Luke 9:1-16) and later He sent out seventy in pairs (Luke 10:1-16). In sending out the disciples, Jesus gave them power and authority over all demons and unclean spirits, to cure diseases, to proclaim the kingdom of God, to preach repentance, to anoint with oil and heal the sick — and they did exactly as they were commissioned.

Supervision — Upon completion of the preaching missions, Jesus made it a point to meet with the disciples ... to hear their reports and to share with them the blessedness of His ministry in doing the same thing. In this sense, one might say that His teaching rotated between instruction and assignment. After the twelve returned from their preaching mission, "they gathered to Jesus and told Him all things both what they had done and what they had taught" (Mark 6:30). Likewise, the seventy returned with joy, reporting that even the demons were subject to them in Jesus' name (Luke 10:17). Jesus responded that He "saw Satan fall like lightning from heaven" (Luke 10:18).

Reproduction — Jesus expected His apostles and disciples to lead individuals to believe in Him, become His disciples, and obey His teachings (Matt. 28:19-20); Mark 16:15; John 17:20-21). In the Upper Room discourse, He shared how He is the true vine and His Father the vinedresser, and every branch in Him that bears fruit would be pruned to bring forth more fruit and much fruit as believers abide in Him (John 15:1-8). Notice in the text how it speaks of fruit, more fruit, and much fruit. Spiritual fruit-bearing is the result of the Holy Spirit's work in man. Coleman notes that "well-intentioned ceremonies, programs, organization, commissions, and crusades of human ingenuity are trying valiantly to do a job that only can be done by people in the power of the Holy Spirit."[2]

Forms and Functions of the Ministry of Jesus

A review of the ministry of Jesus while on earth indicates that He engaged in six forms and functions of ministry to be replicated by the apostles (and certainly by the bishops/elders/pastors who succeeded them):

Praying — Jesus conducted a ministry of prayer beginning with the baptism by John the Baptist (Luke 3:21-22); He prayed all night before He called the disciples who would become apostles (Luke 6:12);

---

2 Coleman, *The Master Plan of Evangelism*, 105.

He taught the disciples how to pray with a model prayer (Matt. 6:5-15, 7:7-12; Luke 11:1-4); He prayed before the disciples after the Upper Room (John 17:1-26); He prayed in the Garden of Gethsemane before His trial and execution (Matt. 26:36-46; Mark 14:32-42; Luke 22:40-46); He was heard praying from the cross (Luke 23:44-46).

Teaching, preaching, healing, and deliverance from Satan's work — His ministry was characterized by teaching, preaching, healing, and delivering those from evil who were demon-possessed (Matt. 4:23, 24). His preaching was from town to town in the synagogues of Galilee. Moved with compassion, He healed and cast out demons (Matt. 9:35-36; Mark 1:38-39, 6:6b). It is interesting to observe that whenever Jesus was "moved with compassion," sickness, diseases, afflictions, demons, and hunger moved out of individuals and multitudes through miraculous healing, deliverance, and provision.

Benevolence — The classic text regarding benevolence and social concern/ministry care is pictured by Jesus returning to earth with His holy angels, at which time He will sit on the throne of glory, and all the nations will be gathered before Him. He will separate them one from another as a shepherd divides the sheep from the goats. The basis for assignment to the place of inheritance in God's kingdom has to do with one's involvement in benevolent activities such as feeding the hungry, giving drink to the thirsty, taking in strangers, clothing people, visiting the sick and those in prison (Matt. 25:31-46). These actions demonstrated true faith. The disciples carried a money bag with funds available for ministry (John 12:6). This is ministry to "the least of these."

Models of Ministry Embraced and Advocated by Jesus

Three models of ministry are implied by what Jesus did and taught as He proclaimed, explained, and demonstrated the message of the kingdom of God:

The Minister as Shepherd — The pastor-shepherd model is the most comprehensive biblical model of pastoral leadership and ministry, and shepherding is the pivotal analogy for pastoral theology. In the Old Testament, the Lord is represented as a good shepherd who takes care of the sheep such that they are content (Ps. 23:1-4, 80:1; Ezek. 34:11-31). Some spiritual leaders in the Old Testament were bad, self-indulgent, shepherds (Jer. 10:21, 23:1-4, 25:34-36; Ezek. 34:1-10). They did not properly care for God's people.

In the New Testament are a host of passages and verses that speak of shepherding as applied to ministry (John 10:1-16, 26-27, 21:15-19; Luke 15:3-7; Acts 20:17-38; Eph. 4:11; 1 Pet. 2:25, 5:1-4). The Gospel according to John records Jesus declaring Himself as the true shepherd who stands in front of the sheep to lead them through the gate to the sheep pen and out of the sheep pen, because the sheep know the shepherd's voice. The good shepherd protects the sheep from wolves and other predators; He cares for the sheep and goes after the lost one until He finds it and then rejoices when He finds it. A good shepherd does not function in an overbearing manner or for dishonest gain; he is an example to the flock.

Jesus could have chosen any number of metaphors to describe church leaders, but he chose "shepherd" or "pastor." Charles Jefferson wrote, "If the aim of our life is to be Christlike, then we must be like a shepherd. If we are called to fulfill Christ's mission, then our work is that of a shepherd ... To glorify Him we must do a shepherd's work, and to enjoy Him forever we must have the shepherd's heart."[3] Richard Baxter, writing in 1656, believed that "every flock should have its own

---

3 Charles Jefferson, *The Minister as Shepherd: The Privileges and Responsibilities of Pastoral Leadership* (Fort Washington, PA: CLS Publications, 2006; originally published 1912), 15. There is not a finer work on shepherding than W. Phillip Keller's *A Shepherd Looks at Psalm 23* (Grand Rapids: Zondervan, 1970, 2007).

pastor, and every pastor his own flock … It is the will of God that every church should have its own pastor … ."[4]

The Minister as a Servant — Jesus was well known for what has come to be called servant leadership, a form of ministry not based upon the leader being served by the followers, but the leader serving the followers. The early disciples of Jesus were not exempt from thinking about positions of prominence, prestige, honor, and earthly power in the kingdom of God as they initially understood it (Matt. 20:20-21; Mark 10:35-37). They had valuable lessons to learn about humility, selfless service, focus on others, and love — qualities that modern pastors and ministers of the gospel must emulate in character and conduct before the people they serve in the name of Jesus.

Aubrey Malphurs, a longtime professor of leadership and pastoral ministry at Dallas Theological Seminary and church consultant through The Malphurs Group (an organization he founded in the 1990s), proposes from Matthew 20:25-28, Mark 10:34-35, and Luke 22:24-30 that servant leaders display four character qualities:

(1) **humility** — servants do not see others beneath them, and they don't lord over, misuse, or abuse their subordinates.

(2) **service** — service is not status; it takes the role of a servant and practices selfless ministry without expecting anything in return.

(3) **focus on others** — ministry is not about self and serving oneself but about care and concern for other people.

(4) **love** — servant leaders will serve others humbly only to the degree that they love them. Love and humility cause us to kneel before those we are serving, as Jesus did when He washed the feet of the disciples.[5]

---

4 Richard Baxter, *The Reformed Pastor* (Carlisle, PA: The Banner of Truth Trust, 1997; originally published 1656), 88.
5 Aubrey Malphurs, *Being Leaders: The Nature of Authentic Christian Leadership* (Grand Rapids: Baker, 2003), 33-42.

Gospel ministers attempt to serve Christ through ministry to people in as many ways as possible. The bottom line is providing compassionate care and concern to the people the minister is serving.

The Minister as a Steward — Another perspective for understanding pastoral ministry and Christian leadership must take into consideration the factor of accountability or responsibility to the Lord. One of the scriptural qualifications for the elder is that he must be a steward of God (Tit. 1:7). A steward in biblical times served as a house manager or administrator-trustee of a household, one who managed the affairs of another. Gospel ministry is a stewardship from God (1 Cor. 9:15).

Those who serve in pastoral leadership and ministry are stewards of God's revelation, trust, and resources (1 Cor. 4:2). Stewards, in a sense, serve in the place of and on behalf of Christ. We must give diligent care to each of God's assigned duties in ministry, knowing that we serve churches and people with first-line accountability to our Lord. Someday we will give account of our works and ministries at the judgment seat of Christ (Rom. 14:10; 1 Cor. 3:8-15; 2 Cor. 5:9-11).

Jesus used several parables about stewards to teach His disciples about responsibility, loyalty, and faithfulness in the work of God:

Luke 16:1-13 — How we handle material resources entrusted to us is a good indication of how responsible we will be in handling God's true spiritual riches.

Matthew 25:14-30 — One day we will be called upon to give an account of our stewardship in relation to our faithfulness with what God has entrusted us with.

Matthew 20:1-16 — The true owner of the vineyard is the Lord; the steward is an overseer or manager on behalf of the owner in relation to the requirements and expectations of the owner.

Hebrews 13:7, 17, and 24 remind spiritual leaders who lead God's people that they must give account for their ministries. Those who serve in an official teaching and preaching role in the church are warned of stricter judgment in James 3:1, warning the prospective teacher of the role's sacredness and seriousness. I remember times that it has really affected me when people died that I preached to and taught, and I asked myself, "Did I preach and teach what they needed to hear and know in order to go to heaven and live a triumphant victorious life as a Christian until they get there?"

Ministers are stewards of what God has entrusted to them, beginning with His Word, the empowerment of His Holy Spirit, and the spiritual gifts that have been given the minister of the gospel.

CHAPTER 3

GIFTED CHRISTIANS IN MINISTRY

In 1 Peter 4:10-11, the Apostle Peter writes that a believer in Christ should use whatever gift (or gifts) he or she has received to minister to others. Whether one's gift is speaking or serving, it should be done with the strength God provides, that He may be glorified and praised through Jesus Christ.

The gift ministry appears to have followed the pouring out of the Holy Spirit at Pentecost in Jerusalem, foretold in Joel 2:28-30. Peter is certainly referring to spiritual gifts the Apostle Paul wrote about in Romans 12:6-8; 1 Corinthians 12:8-10, 28-30; and Ephesians 4:11. These gifts are divinely bestowed by the Lord in His grace, and they cannot be earned or merited. The gifts are for the purpose of edification, exhortation, evangelism, and consolation in the church.

The gift of pastor and teacher — like that of apostle, prophet, and evangelist — is a spiritual leadership gift given by Christ to the church when He ascended on high (Eph. 4:7-11) for preparing the Body of Christ for service and maturing those within the church. Romans 11:29 reminds us that the "gifts and calling of God are irrevocable." God does not change His mind with reference to His calling.

What an honor it is to serve Christ and His church as a pastor with the spiritual gifts He has entrusted the Christian with! May God bless your study of the Word of God and preparation for the pastorate! Paul wrote about this honor: "Let the elders who rule well be counted worthy of double honor, especially those who labor in the word and doctrine. For the Scripture says, 'You shall not muzzle an ox while it treads out the grain,' and 'the laborer is worthy of his wages'" (1 Tim. 5:17-18). The honored privilege of using the spiritual gifts in preaching and teaching the Word of God in ministry and pastoring a church deserves to be compensated by the people of Christ.

Spiritual Gifts

The New Testament speaks of a ministry and leadership ability as a spiritual gift, χάρισμα *(charisma)* or gifts, χαρίσματα *(charismata)*, an endowment or extraordinary ability or power given by the Holy Spirit to churches via individuals (Rom. 12:6-8; 1 Cor. 12:8-10, 28; Eph. 4:11; 1 Pet. 4:11). These endowments are gifts of God's grace necessary for the church to fulfill the mission Christ left for the church. The gifts differ from the fruit of the Spirit (Gal. 5:22-23).

The general categories of the Spiritual Gifts are:

Speaking gifts — in which God's message goes forth in understandable language.

Serving gifts — in which God's love and care for people is demonstrated.

Sign gifts — in which God's power and authority are manifested to substantiate the message.

The gifts in Romans 12:6-8, 1 Corinthians 12:8-10, 28, and 1 Peter 4:11 are the following:

Prophecy — the ability to proclaim God's message, to speak a word from the Lord; it may have a predictive aspect to it, but not necessarily; forth-telling (declarative) and foretelling (predictive).

Ministry — service to others; unselfish and Christlike care for people.

Teaching — instructing believers, especially in the teaching of Jesus (Matt. 28:20) and the Apostles Doctrine (Acts 2:42), via the Word of God (2 Tim. 3:16).

Exhortation — the ability to inspire, urge, persuade, encourage, admonish, or warn, especially when speaking about theological, moral, and spiritual matters.

Giving — generosity or liberality in giving to others in need or in supporting God's work.

Ruling — leadership, taking the lead to guide and direct God's people and His work; leadership under Christ, not "lording" over the flock; an executive administrative ability given by God.

Showing mercy — acts of kindness in helping the poor and needy, visiting the sick, counseling the troubled, and comforting those in sorrow — a cheerful personality is needed, not a gloomy, negative, and pessimistic countenance.

Wisdom — words of wisdom or applied truth out of the context of righteousness, holiness, and love — biblical and Christ-centered applied truth.

Knowledge — words of knowledge out of the mind of Christ and the Word of God; sanctified intelligence; an understanding of the things of God; this is the knowledge of truth by which people are sanctified and set free from bondage.

Faith — the ability to believe God for great things that glorify God; a confidence in God that emboldens one to attempt difficult and seemingly impossible things for God.

Healings — gifts of cures, not limited to miraculous interventions but also cooperating with God's laws for healing. God is the healer but uses individuals and prayer as instruments of His healing (Acts 5:14-16; James 5:13-18).

Miracles — the ability to perform extraordinary works through

God's power (see John 14:12 and Acts 2:43, 4:29-30, 14:3; Rom. 15:18-19; 2 Cor. 12:12; Heb. 2:4).

Discernment — the ability to discern spirits, distinguishing between true and false prophecies and spirits.

Tongues — the ability to speak God's word in different languages under the inspiration of the Holy Spirit as in Acts 2, so that God's Word is transported across language barriers; some Christians understand this to include an unknown prayer language.

Interpretation of tongues — the ability to translate and interpret (give meaning) to languages not understood by the people.

Gifts in Ephesians 4:11 tied to positions and offices/functions in the church:

Apostles — take the teachings of Christ as missionaries to places where Christ is not known as witnesses of the resurrection power of Christ. To be selected as an apostle to replace Judas, one had to have been with Jesus from the beginning of His ministry and be a witness of the resurrection — in that sense no one would qualify today.

Prophets — speak on behalf of the Lord with the authority of God and Christ as preachers of God's word.

Evangelists — share the saving truths of the gospel message to lost and unsaved people to facilitate conversion by God's Word and Spirit.

Pastors* — shepherd the Body of Christ (the church); shepherding implies leading, feeding, healing, protecting, rescuing, and loving the people of God.

Teachers* — instruct people in the teachings of Christ and the Scriptures; facilitate understanding and application of God's Word.

*Some Greek scholars see the Greek construction of ποιμένας (poimenas) καὶ διδασκάλους (didaskalous) as pastor-teachers.

Seven Purposes of Spiritual Gifts
1. To assist believers in worship
2. To empower believers and churches
3. To equip believers for works of service
4. To build up the church, the Body of Christ
5. To encourage and equip believers in evangelism
6. To enlighten believers about God's purpose for them
7. To meet the needs of people with God's resources[1]

Qualities and Qualifications of the Pastoral Office

The two key passages laying out the qualities and qualifications for pastoral ministry are listed in 1 Timothy 3:1-7 and Titus 1:5-9. Since there is considerable overlap between the two passages, a merged list is offered with the profile necessary for pastoral candidates and officers in churches.

Above reproach (1 Tim. 3:2; Tit. 1:6) — blameless; a spotless character such that no one can lay a charge upon you that would cast reproach on the cause of Christ or His church. Your reputation, since conversion to Christ, is marked by moral fidelity and integrity. No grounds exist for accusing this man of immoral or improper conduct.

The husband of one wife (1 Tim. 3:2; Tit. 1:6) — A pastor is literally to be a *mias gynaikos andra (anēr)*, a one-woman man. A blameless man is morally, spiritually, and sexually faithful to one woman. Nothing is said about divorce; however, remarriage to a Christian woman is possible for a bishop, elder, or pastor whose wife has died (1 Cor. 7:39).

Temperate (1 Tim. 3:2; Tit. 1:8) — self-controlled. An orderly, disciplined life. Clearheaded, avoiding excesses; well-balanced, calm, careful, steady, and sane. Emotions stay in check. One is not in bondage to self and the desires of the flesh.

---

1 Source of this list not known.

Sober-minded (1 Tim. 3:2; Tit. 1:8) — sensible, of sound mind, reasonable, serious, keeps one's head. The idea is discreet, prudent, cautious, avoiding foolish behavior, balanced in judgment. Not given to quick and superficial decisions based on immature thinking.

Of good behavior (1 Tim. 3:2) — respectable, honorable, suggesting a life that is organized and not chaotic; a well-ordered life, worthy of respect.

Hospitable (1 Tim. 3:2; Tit. 1:8) — shows kindness to strangers; unselfish and shares blessings with others. People are welcome in your presence and home.

Able to teach (1 Tim. 3:2) — a primary duty of church leaders is teaching, instructing in the faith. Able to communicate God's truth to people and exhort sound doctrine in a way that is not argumentative. Deacons are not required to be able to teach.

Not given to wine (1 Tim. 3:3; Tit. 1:7) — not addicted to wine. Literally, the idea in Greek is one who does not sit long at the wine. Drunkenness is a sin of the flesh, and alcohol can affect one's moral reasoning and judgment. Abstinence is the best position for pastors who desire to be wise and filled with the Holy Spirit (Luke 1:15; Eph. 5:15-21).

Not violent (1 Tim. 3:3; Tit. 1:7) — not given to physical violence; not contentious, not looking for a fight.

But gentle (1 Tim. 3:3) — kind, yielding, forbearing, characterized by graciousness and tenderness.

Not quarrelsome (1 Tim. 3:3) — peaceable. The idea here is not disposed to fight; not contentious.

Not greedy for money (1 Tim. 3:3; Tit. 1:7) — not a lover of money, not stingy; literally not a friend or lover of silver; free from the love of money.

Not covetous — not fond of or eager for dishonest gain and not desiring what belongs to others.

**Rules his own house well, having his children in submission with all reverence, for if a man does not know how to rule his own house, how

will he take care of the church of God? (1 Tim. 3:4-5) — a good leader in one's own home, ruling his own household well. If a man's own children do not obey and respect him, then his church is not likely to follow his leadership very seriously. The pastor cannot be one thing at home and something else in the church. He has the respect of his family and is the recognized leader of his home. This does not mean he is entitled to be a dictator in the home or church and will make all the decisions. A pastor is not going to lead the church any better than he leads his own family.

Having faithful children not accused of dissipation or insubordination (Tit. 1:6) — children not accused of debauchery, dissipation, profligacy, or incorrigibility; having believing children that are not accused of being unruly and disorderly but are obedient and respectful of authority.

Not a novice, lest being puffed up with pride he falls into the same condemnation as the devil (1 Tim. 3:6) — not a new convert, a neophyte, but a mature believer who has been a Christian for a significant length of time — at least long enough to demonstrate the reality of his conversion and depth of spirituality. He must certainly understand the basic teachings of Christ and the apostles and have a consistency in Christlike character and good judgment. A new Christian is not qualified to lead the church.

A good testimony among those who are outside, lest he fall into reproach and the snare of the devil (1 Tim. 1:7) — a reputation for honesty in character, conduct, and integrity outside the church throughout the community. A bad reputation leaves a church leader and the church open to reproach and the snare (trap) of the devil.

A steward of God (Tit. 1:7) — God's manager, administrator. A steward does not own but manages all his master puts into his hands. He manages God's resources wisely. He sees himself accountable to God for ministry and resources.

Not self-willed (Tit. 1:7) — not stubborn, arrogant; not one who lives to please himself and is willful, obstinate, or imperious.

Not quick-tempered (Tit. 1:7) — not inclined to anger; not irascible; able to control one's temper.

A lover of what is good (Tit. 1:8) — a lover of the good, goodness, and good men. He must not love what is evil and sinful. What is good honors and glorifies God, since God is ultimate goodness.

Just (Tit. 1:8) — upright, just, righteous; one who does what is right in God's sight. He makes wise and sound judgments based upon the principles of God's Word.

Holy (Tim. 1:8) — means devout, pious, pleasing to God; set apart and separated unto God in righteous character and conduct.

Holding fast the faithful word as he has been taught, that he may be able by sound doctrine both to exhort and convict those who contradict (Tit. 1:9) — holds fast to the truth of God's Word and is able to exhort and encourage others to believe it and obey it. A faithful teacher of God's Word corrects those who are in error regarding the teachings of Christ and the apostles.

The Holy Spirit's Filling for Pastoral Ministry

Spiritual leadership requires Spirit-filled people. Other qualities are important; to be Spirit-filled is indispensable. Without spirituality, a pastor and ministry leader are incapable of giving truly spiritual leadership. The Spirit-filled believer is the divine ideal in ministry and spiritual leadership. Jesus, our example, was "full of the Spirit" (Luke 4:1), having received the Holy Spirit without measure (John 3:34). When full of the Holy Spirit, Jesus was led by the Spirit and empowered by the Holy Spirit to resist temptation (Luke 4:1-13). Each member of the family of Zacharias, Elizabeth, and John were "filled with the Spirit" (Luke 1:15, 41, 67), and the disciples and others were filled again and again after their anointed ministries had begun after Pentecost (Acts 2:4; 4:8, 31; 6:3; 7:55; 9:17; 11:24; 13:52). In the Acts of the Apostles, there are fifty-six references to the Holy Spirit at work in the lives of followers of Jesus.

Jesus promised that the Holy Spirit would flow out of a believer's heart like rivers of living water (John 7:37-39). This is the prerogative of every Christian, but, sadly, many church members and even some pastors seem to know very little about a Spirit-filled life and ministry. Yet, a Christian, to be spiritually minded, empowered, and directed, must then be filled and kept filled by the Spirit. Ephesians 5:18 says, "Be filled with the Spirit." The present imperative of the Greek verb has the sense of keep on being filled. To be filled with the Spirit is not the issue of believers getting more of the Spirit; it is rather the matter of the Spirit getting more of us. We already have all the Holy Spirit we will ever get, but He may not have all of us yet.

The Holy Spirit's presence and power are a reality in our lives when we are Spirit-filled believers. The Holy Spirit will not delegate authority into secular or carnal hands, even when a particular job has no direct spiritual teaching involved; all workers must be Spirit-led and Spirit-filled. The Bible nowhere provides a neat, concise formula for being filled with the Spirit of God. Billy Graham wrote, "I believe that [the fact that there is no neat, concise formula] may be because most believers in the first century did not need to be told how to be filled. They knew that the Spirit-filled life was the normal Christian life."[2]

Christians may indeed be filled with the Holy Spirit (Eph. 5:18; cf. Luke 1:15, 41, 6:7; 4:1; Acts 2:4; 4:8; 6:3, 5; 7:55; 9:17; 11:24; 13:9). Wayne Grudem said in a sermon, "To be filled with the Holy Spirit is to be

---

2 Billy Graham, *The Holy Spirit: Activating God's Power in Your Life* (Waco: Word, 1978), 109.

filled with the immediate presence of God himself, and it therefore will result in feeling what God feels, desiring what God desires, doing what God wants, speaking by God's power, praying and ministering in God's strength, and knowing with the knowledge which God himself gives. In times when the church experiences revival, the Holy Spirit produces these results in people's lives in especially powerful ways."[3] Therefore, in our Christian lives and pastoral ministry, it is important that we depend on the Holy Spirit's power, recognizing that any significant work is done "not by might, nor by power, but by my Spirit, says the Lord of hosts" (Zech. 4:6).

To be filled with the Holy Spirit, we must certainly desire the Holy Spirit to fill us. The Holy Spirit does not take control of anyone against his or her will. The Acts of the Apostles clearly demonstrates that leaders who significantly influenced people in the earliest days of the church were Spirit-filled. The early leaders of the church had surrendered their own wills to the Spirit's control; they were sensitive to the leading of the Spirit of God. J. Oswald Sanders wrote, "The Holy Spirit does not take control of any man or body of men against their will. When He sees men elected to positions of leadership who lack spiritual fitness to cooperate with Him, He quietly withdraws and leaves them to implement their own policy according to their own standards, but without His aid. The inevitable issue is an unspiritual administration."[4] God will not fill us with His Spirit against our will and inward desires. Therefore, we must ask God for an infilling of the Holy Spirit and not look for any kind of outward signs or manifestations. The way in which we ask God for a full measure of His Spirit is through prayer (Matt. 7:7-11; Luke 11:9-13).

---

[3] Wayne Grudem, "Being Filled with the Holy Spirit" (notes from a sermon), accessed 2 June 2021, https://realityventura.s3.amazonnews.com.
[4] J. Oswald Sanders, *Spiritual Leadership: Principles of Excellence for Every Believer* (Chicago: Moody Press, 1994), 80.

This is an act of faith and obedience (Eph. 5:18), a condition resulting from faith, not a feeling or impulse or gush of inward and outer enthusiasm. The one hundred and twenty disciples, after the ascension of Jesus, were baptized and filled with the Holy Spirit after continuing prayer and supplication in the upper room in Jerusalem (Acts 1:12-14, 2:1-4).

To be filled with God's Spirit, we must empty ourselves of anything that would hinder God's Spirit from filling our vessel and flowing through us. Philippians 2:7 reminds us that Jesus "emptied Himself" when He became incarnate; that is, He laid aside the glory He had with His Heavenly Father and came to earth as a man, taking the form of a servant. For us redeemed sinners to empty ourselves, we must divest ourselves of everything in our vessel that does not belong there by confessing sin (1 John 1:9), forsaking sin (Isa. 55:7), and repenting (Acts 3:19-20) of all known sin in our lives, surrendering ourselves totally and irrevocably (Rom. 12:1-2) to the lordship of Jesus Christ in everything (Luke 6:46).

This means yielding ourselves completely to God and His will. This means checking our motives and making sure our intentions are pure and holy. Billy Graham reminds us that it is not easy to deal honestly and completely with every known sin in our lives: "This may be very painful for us, as we face up to things that we have hidden or not even realized about our lives. But there will be no filling by the Holy Spirit apart from cleansing from sin, and the first step in cleansing from sin is awareness of its presence."[5] This further means that we must reckon (regard, consider) ourselves dead unto sin but alive unto God through Jesus Christ our Lord (Rom. 6:11), an indication that we are "crucified with Christ" (Gal. 2:20).

Consequently, we must allow the work of the Holy Spirit to cleanse

---

5 Graham, *The Holy Spirit*, 110.

us spiritually and morally and renew our purposes toward God through repentance; otherwise, the fire of God's judgment will burn up the chaff of unrepentant lives (Matt. 3:1-12, Luke 3:7-18). If believers will be cleansed and filled with the Holy Spirit, we must judge ourselves and turn from our sins or else we will be chastened by the Lord (1 Cor. 11:31-32, Heb. 12:3-11).

Furthermore, we will know that we are filled with the Holy Spirit because we will have power to speak boldly the Word of God and to witness and testify on behalf of Jesus Christ (Acts 1:8; 2:1-13; 4:8-12, 31; 13:9-12). We will have a singing, thankful, and submissive heart (Eph. 5:19-21) and the joy of the Lord (Acts 13:52). We will be led by the Spirit of God (Rom. 8:14, Gal. 1:8), walk in the Spirit (Rom. 8:4-5; Gal. 5:16, 25), bear the fruit of the Spirit (Gal. 5:22-24), and speak truth in which Jesus Christ is glorified (John 16:13-15). And we will take a stand and influence people as Peter did at Pentecost (Acts 2:14-47).

The Apostle Paul wrote to the Ephesians, "Do not get drunk with wine, for that is debauchery; but be filled with the Spirit" (Eph. 5:18). J. Edwin Orr in *Full Surrender* comments succinctly on this verse: "In alcoholic intoxication, a man is possessed by an alien spirit: a quiet man becomes rowdy, a mean man becomes generous, a decent man becomes bestial, a cautious man becomes reckless: and folks excuse him by saying that he is not himself, he is intoxicated. The filling of the Holy Spirit is God-intoxication; not fanaticism, but the possession of a man's faculties by the Holy Spirit of God, whereby his acts resemble acts of a Divine Being, who possesses him. The fruit of the Spirit is the very opposite of extravagance or fanaticism."[6]

Finally, Sanders makes it quite plain, "To be filled with the Spirit means simply that the Christian voluntarily surrenders life and will to

---

6 J. Edwin Orr, *Full Surrender* (London: Marshall, Morgan & Scott, 1951), 116.

the Spirit. Through faith, the believer's personality is filled, mastered, and controlled by the Spirit. The meaning of 'filled' is not 'to pour into a passive container' but 'to take possession of the mind.' That's the meaning found in Luke 5:26: 'They were filled with awe.' When we invite the Spirit to fill us, the Spirit's power grips our lives with this kind of strength and passion."[7]

Sanders concludes, "To be filled with the Spirit is to be controlled by the Spirit. The Christian leader's mind, emotions, will, and physical strength all become available for the Spirit to guide and use. Under the Spirit's control, natural gifts of leadership are lifted to their highest power, sanctified for holy purpose. Through the work of the now ungrieved and unhindered Spirit, all the fruits of the Spirit start to grow in the leader's life. His witness is more winsome, service more steady, and testimony more powerful. All real Christian service is but the expression of the Spirit's power through believers yielded to Him (John 7:37-39). … The filling of the Spirit is essential for spiritual leadership. And each of us is as full of the Spirit as we really want to be."[8]

Literature on the Filling of the Spirit for Ministry

Below you will find some excellent books on the filling of the Holy Spirit for Christian life and ministry that point the reader to the Word of God.

- Criswell, W.A. *The Baptism, Filling & Gifts of the Holy Spirit*. Grand Rapids: Zondervan, 1973.
- _____. *The Holy Spirit in Today's World*. Grand Rapids: Zondervan, 1966.

---

7 Sanders, *Spiritual Leadership*, 81-82.
8 Ibid., 82.

- Graham, Billy. *The Holy Spirit: Activating God's Power in Your Life*. Waco: Word, 1978.
- Grudem, Wayne. "The Work of the Holy Spirit" and "Baptism in and Filling with the Holy Spirit" in *Systematic Theology*. Grand Rapids: Zondervan, 1994.
- Meyer, F.B. *The Christ-Life for the Self-Life*. Chicago: Moody Press, n.d.
- Orr, J. Edwin. *Full Surrender*. London: Marshall, Morgan & Scott, 1951.
- Paxson, Ruth. *Rivers of Living Water*. Chicago: Moody, n.d.
- Torrey, R.A. *How to Obtain Fullness of Power*. Springdale, PA: Whitaker House, n.d.

CHAPTER 4

CHOSEN TO SERVE JESUS IN GOSPEL MINISTRY

In John 15:16, Jesus, in the Upper Room, told the Twelve, "You did not choose Me, but I chose you and appointed [ordained (KJV)] you that you should go and bear fruit, that your fruit should remain, that whatever you ask the Father in My name He may give you." In Mark 3:14-15, we read how Jesus "appointed [ordained (KJV)] twelve, that they might be with Him and that He might send them out to preach, and to have power to heal sicknesses, and to cast out demons." This calling and selection was a special setting aside of twelve disciples who were called apostles to be the first spiritual leaders of the church from all the other disciples who followed Jesus.

Disciples normally chose the rabbi they wanted to be attached to, but this was not so with Jesus's disciples. He chose them for a purpose: They were to go and bear abiding spiritual fruit by preaching, teaching, healing, and casting out demons. These apostles have long since served their gospel ministry calling from Christ and have gone on to their eternal reward. If you have been called to prepare for pastoral ministry, you are preparing to take your place in a long line of gospel ministers appointed to shepherd the church of God (Acts 20:28).

The Apostle Paul, in his first letter to Timothy, wrote, "I was appointed [ordained (KJV)] a preacher and an apostle … a teacher of the Gentiles in faith and truth" (1 Tim. 2:7). Paul understood his calling to evangelize, disciple, and plant churches that would need pastors called elders, which he and Barnabas appointed in every church on the first missionary journey (Acts 14:23). You can rejoice today in that Christ has chosen you to prepare to serve Him as a pastor with ministry to people who need to hear the wonderful story of the gospel that saves the soul unto life eternal.

This chapter will deal with licensure and ordination to the gospel ministry in churches. Different denominations and churches handle the path toward ordination a little differently, but the bottom line is that the church validates, authenticates, and commissions a fully qualified candidate through ordination to serve God and His people in ministry.

Licensure to the Gospel Ministry

Licensure is not a biblical practice referred to in Scripture except as it facilitates the opportunity for one to prove himself as to ability and character in preparation for ordination. First Timothy 3:10 speaks of deacons first being proved (tested) for character and conduct before serving — how much more so, gospel ministers.

The practice of licensing allows the church to publicly recognize a call to the gospel ministry and at the same time comply with the New Testament injunction of 1 Timothy 5:22: "Do not lay hands on anyone hastily." Unfortunately, I have heard of churches moving to license or ordain a talented man with speaking gifts too quickly, often to the embarrassment of the congregation.

Generally, a prospective prospect for vocational Christian ministry will let the church know of his calling, either through meeting with a pastor or in the Baptist tradition of going forward during the time of invitation at the close of the worship service when he announces his calling to the church. This is the way I did it at my home church.

Thereafter, I began meeting with the pastor of the church where my wife and I were members and staying in contact with my home church pastor. Next, I volunteered to do church visitation on a weekday night, and in time the pastor called and offered me the opportunity to preach at one of the church's mission chapels in view of the possibility of becoming the pastor of that mobile home park congregation. The chapel people did select me to be their pastor, a decision confirmed by the church. Not long afterward, my home church had me come back to preach in a Sunday morning worship service and be licensed to the gospel ministry.

Typical procedures toward licensing in Baptist and other evangelical churches include: (1) The congregation votes to license a candidate in a regular business meeting after hearing the individual's testimony and recommendation of the pastor and deacons; (2) churches will often have the individual preach at a regular worship service, then afterward there will be a prayer and presentation of the certificate of license, with a ministry gift given like a set of commentaries. I received my first set of commentaries at this service. It may not happen this way in megachurches.

Some churches on the certificate of license write or type an end date (most often one year or a stipulated time), but my church did not do that. As I was in the military at the time and in seminary afterward, I served as a licensed minister for seven years before ordination, doing ministry as a mission pastor, youth minister, single adult minister, and a chapel pastor again before receiving a call to serve a fourteen-month interim pastorate at an established church. As I was thirty years old like Jesus was about thirty when He began His formal ministry (Luke 3:23), I came to believe the time was right, and my home church ordained me on a Sunday after meeting with an ordination committee on Saturday night.

Licensure has its roots in England when itinerant preachers were required by the Church of England to have a license to preach granted by bishops in their diocese. A man could not legally preach in a pulpit without a license. John Bunyan, a Nonconformist deacon, began preaching in 1655, was indicted in 1658 for preaching without a license, then was imprisoned from 1660-1672 for preaching without a license. He was imprisoned again in 1675 for the same offense. While in prison the first time, he wrote his autobiography *Grace Abounding to the Chief of Sinners* and began *The Pilgrim's Progress*, which was not published until some years after his release.

In America, preachers have been licensed by churches and denominations as a first step toward ordination. This is understood as an opportunity to demonstrate to the church one's faithfulness to Christ, the Scriptures, and to begin preaching and conducting ministry as the Lord opens the door with the blessing of the church.

Ordination to the Gospel Ministry

All Christians are called to discipleship and to share in Christ's ministry in a general sense. But only a few are called and set aside to ordained gospel ministry. These individuals have been duly called by God, prepared, examined, ordained, and authorized by a church for a representative Christian ministry on behalf of the church or denomination.

Ordination has its roots in a "laying on of hands" observance going back to Old Testament times in recognition of the call, commissioning, and installation of a representative of the Lord. Deuteronomy 34:9 and Numbers 27:18-23 speak of Moses laying his hands upon Joshua for leadership.

In New Testament times, individuals were ordained (set apart) to spiritual leadership and ministry as overseers, elders, pastors, or deacons in local churches. This action of the church is referred to in Acts 6:6 (the apostles laid hands on the men selected by the church for their ministry). First Timothy 4:14 speaks of the presbytery (elders) laying hands on Timothy.

Timothy's commissioning to ministry leadership referred to in 1 Timothy 4:14 was confirmed:

A. *subjectively* (by means of a spiritual gift observed by Christians);

B. *objectively* (through the prophecy made about him); and

C. *collectively* (by the affirmation of apostles and the church, as represented by the elders).

Hands were not to be laid on "hastily" — without thorough investigation of qualifications (1 Tim. 5:22). The New Testament speaks of ordination as appointment to ministry. Jesus "ordained" or "appointed" His disciples (John 15:16) for fruit-bearing spiritual leadership and ministry. He "appointed" the Twelve to be with Him, to go out and preach, to have authority to heal sicknesses and cast out demons (Mark 3:14; Matt. 19:1; Luke 9:1).

Paul was "ordained" or "appointed" as a preacher and an apostle (1 Tim. 2:7). He told the Ephesian elders that the Holy Spirit had "made" them overseers to shepherd the church of God, which He purchased with His own blood (Acts 20:28).

On his first missionary journey, Paul and Barnabas "appointed" elders in every church after prayer, fasting, and commending them to the Lord to serve as spiritual leaders in the churches (Acts 14:23). Paul instructed Titus to "appoint" elders in the cities of Crete (Titus 1:5). Qualifications for appointment to the office are listed in Titus 1:6-9 and 1 Timothy 3:1-7 that deal with character, conduct, capabilities, creed, and commitment.

The ordination or appointment to the office was a public recognition by the church of the individual's calling and commissioning to spiritual leadership and ministry. Paul taught that the elders were to be regarded as worthy of double honor: respect and financial support

(1 Tim. 5:17). Nothing is ever said about apostolic authority being transferred as taught by some denominations. I remember hearing a well-known pastor and Bible teacher many years ago say, "Nothing is transferred in the laying on of hands but germs." The laying on of hands recognizes a calling from Christ and an appointment by the church.

Steps toward ordination:

- A definite call from the Lord to a preaching, teaching, or ministry recognized by the church.
- Meet the qualifications of 1 Timothy 3:1-7 and Titus 1:5-9, including a commitment to and understanding of sound doctrine.
- Some ministry training and preparation under godly leaders who are sound in faith (2 Tim. 2:2).
- An ordaining council convenes to examine the candidate (1 Tim. 4:14) — a presbytery of elders and deacons to review the candidate's conversion, baptism, church membership, service, calling, character, reputation, qualifications consistent with the godly Christian life, and understanding of doctrine.
- Generally, today in Baptist and independent evangelical churches, upon satisfactory review of the candidate, an ordaining council recommends the ordination of the candidate to the church, which then votes to proceed with a special ordination service when hands will be laid on the candidate.
- Regardless of what goes on at the ordination service, the candidate kneels (or sits) before the church and all ordained pastors, elders, and deacons lay hands on the candidate (Acts 6:6; 13:3; 1 Tim. 5:22). This is the "ordination," or "consecration," or "setting apart," or "the setting aside" of God's servant (1 Tim. 4:4). The "laying on of hands" is usually done by the pastors, elders, and deacons present, but some churches

- allow other church members to lay on hands and pray for the candidate also.
- Typically in our day in churches, there will be an ordination prayer, a charge to the candidate (as in 2 Tim. 4:1-5), perhaps a charge to the church, the presentation of a Bible and an ordination certificate, benediction, and the right hand of fellowship and encouragement by church members and visitors present.

The Ordination of Women as Pastors

The question of women in ministry is not an issue among Baptists and evangelicals. However, the issue of women being ordained to serve as pastors and deacons of local churches is an issue of concern for many Christians in churches and denominations. The college, seminary, and university where I have taught and currently teach do not ordain anyone for ministry and welcome men and women to ministry degree programs. Professors have their own convictions about the ordination of women.

For arguments in support of ordaining women, see Thomas Oden, *Pastoral Theology: Essentials of Ministry*, 35-46; for arguments not to ordain women, see John MacArthur and the Master's Seminary Faculty, *Pastoral Ministry: How to Shepherd Biblically*, 107-117.

Arguments *for* the ordination of women:

1. Thomas Oden interprets Philippians 4:2-3 that women were involved in positions of leadership in the early church.

2. Paul lists several women (Phoebe, Prisca, Mary, Tryphaena, Tryphosa, and Julia) in Romans 16:1-16 alongside men as "fellow workers in Christ." Oden interprets these as not in subordinate positions to men in the church.

3. Oden rejects the historical practice and tradition of the church

ordaining men only to serve as bishops, elders, pastors, and deacons, believing the church was in error regarding this practice.

4. Oden's view is based on four streams of thought (Scripture, tradition, reason, and experience); he believes there is no compelling theological reason why women should be viewed as incapable of ministerial orders.

5. Oden rejects the texts regarding women being subject to their own husbands (1 Cor. 11:3; Eph. 5:22-24; Col. 3:18) as "problematic."

6. Oden cites Gal. 3:28, which speaks of "neither male nor female; for you are all one in Christ Jesus," as reflecting "an amazingly equalitarian [egalitarian] view of men and women in Christ" that he applies to ordination. Oden writes, "We have no warrant to conclude that God is male." Oden says, "The shepherding image is a parenting image, just as applicable to women as men, and perhaps even more so. In the human past, women have cared for flocks just as often and well as men."

One of the earliest ordinations of a Baptist woman occurred in 1877 when two Michigan Freewill Baptist churches listed Lura Mains as an ordained minister. Later, she organized and served as pastor of a Freewill Baptist church in Branch County, Michigan. The first ordination of a Northern Baptist (now American Baptist) woman, May Jones, took place in 1882. Within Southern Baptist circles, Addie Davis was the first ordained woman. Watts Street Baptist Church in Durham, North Carolina, ordained her in 1964, and she pastored in Vermont and Rhode Island.

In 2008, about 600 women served as pastors or co-pastors of Baptist churches in America. The majority were affiliated with the American Baptist Churches, USA, with eleven women then serving as pastors of Baptist churches in Texas. Churches affiliated with the National Baptist Convention, USA, Inc.; Progressive National Baptist Convention,

Inc.; Cooperative Baptist Fellowship; Alliance of Baptists; and Baptist General Convention of Texas have ordained women as pastors. There have been a few churches of the 47,530 congregations in the Southern Baptist Convention that have ordained a very small number of women (each church is independent and autonomous and is not controlled by the denomination).

Arguments *against* the ordination of women:

1. Jesus selected twelve men to serve as apostles, the first spiritual leaders of the church. There were women who followed Jesus (Luke 8:1-3), were at the cross (Matt. 27:55, 56; Mark 15:40, 41; John 19:25), and were in the Upper Room prayer meetings (Acts 1:12-14). However, there is no scriptural evidence that women were chosen or proposed to serve as apostles, bishops, elders, pastors, or deacons in the early church.

2. Women were never set apart to the priesthood in Israel, despite pagan religions surrounding the nation that did have religious priestesses. Women in Israel did function as prophetesses, Deborah served as a judge, Esther was a Persian queen, but women did not serve as priestesses.

3. Women certainly served as ministers in the early church (Rom. 16:1-2) as was the case of Phoebe who ministered, Lydia whose home was the first location of the church in Philippi (Acts 16:14-15, 40), and Priscilla who with her husband Aquila instructed Apollos about the Christian faith more accurately (Acts 18:24-26), but women did not serve as pastors (overseers, elders) and deacons. Women did serve as ecclesial deaconesses in early churches beginning in the second and third centuries, according to church history, but were not considered officers of the church and were not ordained to this role.

4. First Timothy 3:2 and Titus 1:6 stipulate that the candidate for the office of overseer and elder be "the husband of one wife." A woman

cannot be the husband of one wife.

5. Only men were ordained to the pastoral office for hundreds of years, a tradition linked strongly to the passed-down teaching and practices of the apostles and those who followed them. Those who advocate women serving as pastors obviously believe that all who have opposed the practice of women serving as overseers, elders, pastors, and deacons from Jesus and the apostles to the present day have been in the dark and were wrong in what they believed, practiced, and taught.

While some Baptist churches have ordained women to serve as pastors and deacons, in the *2000 Baptist Faith & Message*, Southern Baptists oppose ordination of women as pastors with this statement: "Its scriptural officers are pastors and deacons. While both men and women are gifted for service in the church, the office of pastor is limited to men as qualified by Scripture." The statement does not speak to the ordination of women as deacons or deaconesses.

The policy of the National Baptist Convention of America, the second-largest African American Baptist denomination, also opposes ordaining women as pastors.

CHAPTER 5

JESUS AND THE ORDINANCES

In Acts 2:41, we read that upon hearing Peter's message about Jesus being Lord and Christ, about 3,000 souls, after the exhortation to repent and be baptized for the remission of sins, were baptized and added to the Body of Christ. In Acts 8:35-39, we read about Philip baptizing the treasurer of Ethiopia and in Acts 10:47-48 Peter ordered the baptism of those gathered in Cornelius's household who believed in Jesus and received the Holy Spirit; in Acts 16:15, we read about Lydia and her household being baptized after hearing Paul and Silas share the gospel; and in Acts 16:31-33, the family of the Philippian jailer were baptized upon hearing the word of the Lord about Jesus from Paul and Silas.

It has been a great joy through the years as a pastor and chaplain to baptize many individuals after sharing the gospel of Christ with them and reviewing the basics of what baptism and following Jesus means. Paul reminded the church at Rome that believers are baptized into Christ Jesus, into His death and raised to walk in newness of life (Rom. 6:3-4). I was baptized the first time at age ten before I surrendered in faith and obedience to the lordship of Christ, so I was rebaptized at age twenty-four for the assurance that I was baptized after conversion to Jesus Christ as Lord and Savior.

First Corinthians 11:23-34 is the passage we most often think about in relation to the Lord's Supper, also called communion, in churches. This observance memorialized the last Passover Meal Jesus had with the disciples the night before He was crucified. Paul wrote that "as often as you eat this bread and drink this cup, you proclaim the Lord's death till He comes" (11:26). The exhortation to the church instructs believers to examine themselves before eating the bread and drinking from the cup. Paul wrote, "For if we would judge ourselves, we would not be judged" (11:31), suggesting that some had taken the Lord's Supper in an unworthy manner and for that reason many were weak and sickly among them and many have died (11:29-30).

Over the years of ministry, it has been a blessing to conduct and participate in communion observances in churches and in military and civilian chapels. The Lord's Supper has been a time for the Body of Christ to remember the significance of the cross and what the crucified life means in terms of Christian fellowship and unity. I hope you have been spiritually enriched during the observance of the Lord's Supper.

Ordinances in the New Testament

Baptists and other evangelical Christians typically have practiced two church observances: Baptism and the Lord's Supper. Some denominations and churches practice the Washing of Feet. Most churches practice marriage ceremonies, prayers for the sick and dying, and ordination services, but these are not considered ordinances.

Churches refer to baptism and the Lord's Supper as ordinances or sacraments. Roman Catholics use the term "sacrament" as a means of grace, one of the seven sacraments of the Roman Catholic Church. Baptists and many evangelical churches only refer to the two observances as ordinances, or that which is commanded or ordered. Jesus commanded the disciples to baptize believers willing to become disciples (Matt. 28:19), and regarding the Lord's Supper, Jesus said, "Do this in remembrance of Me" (Luke 22:17). Here is a good definition of an ordinance: "An ordinance is a practice established by Jesus Christ that commemorates and symbolizes some aspect of His atoning sacrifice or redeeming work. The church is to observe only those rituals that can clearly be shown to have been ordained by Christ in the New Testament."[1]

Believer's Baptism: The Initiatory Rite

The New Testament stipulates the following about baptism as the initiatory rite:

— Baptism as a rite is an outward symbolic act signifying an inward saving work of God in the life of the believer (Acts 8:36-39).

— Baptism is a public profession of faith in Jesus Christ, prerequisite for church membership (Acts 2:47).

— Baptism follows belief in Jesus and a willingness to learn what the apostles taught that Jesus commanded (Matt. 28:19-20).

Baptism was not an option to be considered regarding church membership, but a command to be obeyed. F.F. Bruce writes: "The idea of an unbaptized Christian is simply not entertained in the New Testament."[2] Norman posits: "An unbaptized believer is a foreign concept to the New Testament and is considered antithetical to the teachings of the Bible."[3] In the early church, only believers were immersed and added to the church.

---

1 R. Stanton Norman, *The Baptist Way: Distinctives of a Baptist Church* (Nashville: B&H Publishers, 2005), 130-31.
2 F.F. Bruce, *The Book of Acts, New International Commentary Series* (Grand Rapids: Eerdmans, 1988), 77.
3 Norman, *The Baptist Way*, 140.

The Meaning of Baptism

Christian baptism symbolizes the death, burial, and resurrection of Jesus. It also typifies the Christian's death of the old life, its burial, and resurrection to walk in newness of life in Christ (Rom. 6:4-6; Col. 2:12). Christian baptism is an act of obedience (Acts 2:38), the first step of discipleship (Matt. 28:19-20), and a picture of the washing away of sins (Acts 22:16). Christian baptism identifies a believer with Jesus Christ and His church (Acts 2:41, 47). Baptism as a symbol also points to the believer's future hope that, like Jesus, we, too, will die — but we will be raised to everlasting life.

The Subjects of Baptism

The New Testament knows nothing of infant baptism but that of believers only. Kurt Aland, a Lutheran scholar, gives a definitive answer to the issue when he quotes Adolf Harnack that "the practice of infant baptism begins after this period (the end of the second century)," concurring that "the practice of infant baptism is not demonstrable in the Apostolic and post-Apostolic age. It is true that we hear frequently of the baptism of whole households (e.g. Acts 16:15, 32f, 18:8; 1 Cor. 1:16). But the last passage taken in conjunction with 1 Corinthians 7:14 does not tell in favor of the view that infant baptism was usual at that time."[4]

Aland adds, "The result to which our investigations have so far led remains constant: direct evidence from the church fathers for infant baptism begins in the third century — a phenomenon which we observe in passing can hardly be accidental. Prior to this, we read only of the baptism of adults; infant baptism appears to be excluded, at least so far

---

4 Kurt Aland, *Did the Early Church Baptize Infants?* (Eugene, OR: Wipf and Stock, 1961), 29.

as anything can be inferred from the texts that have come down to us."[5]

Baptism in the New Testament is never by sprinkling or pouring. These were concessions permitted by some pastors of churches. You can read of an early concession in *The Didache*, most likely a second century document: "Baptize in the name of the Father and of the Son and of the Holy Spirit in running water. But if you have no running water, then baptize in some other water; and if you are not able to baptize in cold water, then do so in warm. But if you have neither, then pour water on the head three times in the name of the Father and the Son and the Holy Spirit."[6]

Norman writes, "Baptism in the NT signifies that a person is capable of exercising biblical faith in Christ, repenting of his own sin, and having the capacity to be an obedient, learning disciple of Christ … Baptists, as is the case with all evangelicals, believe that a saving experience with Christ is the prerequisite for baptism. Baptism without a conscious, willful decision to follow Christ is nonsensical. Because baptism symbolizes faith, repentance, surrender, and purity, we believe that the only subjects of baptism are believers who are capable of professing their own faith."[7]

The Effects of Baptism

Baptists, as is the case with most evangelicals, advocate a commemorative or symbolic view of baptism, rejecting any doctrinal interpretations that make baptism spiritually efficacious: "Baptists do not believe that baptism is the cause of regeneration, remits Adamic guilt or sin, imparts spiritual gifts, or other similar ideas. Baptism produces

---

[5] Aland, *Did the Early Church Baptize Infants?*, 70.
[6] *The Didache* in *The Apostolic Fathers in English, Third Edition,* Michael W. Holmes (Grand Rapids: Baker Academic, 2006), 166.
[7] Norman, *The Baptist Way,* 139, 141.

nothing except the blessing of being obedient to Christ."[8]

Baptism does not literally wash away sin, it does not dispense any grace, nor does it "produce repentance or faith, but it does express those realities."[9] The Lord's Supper is a special observance in the church to remember the death of Jesus, to be spiritually cleansed upon confession of sin and repentance, and to share precious Christian fellowship with other believers in Christ.

The Mode of Baptism

Despite various Christian denominations using different modes of baptism, Baptists and other evangelicals from their earliest days have sought to practice what they believe the early church practiced: the immersion of believers in water.

The Greek word *baptizō* means to dip, plunge, or submerge: "This term was used by secular writers to describe the sinking of a ship, drowning, and metaphorically for being completely overwhelmed."[10] Immersion in water is the best picture of the washing away of sins and complete identification with the death, burial, and resurrection of Jesus Christ (Rom. 6:4).

Preparing for Baptism

An early Christian church father, Hippolytus, wrote how candidates were prepared for baptism, using the Apostle's Creed with some three years of doctrinal preparation and then "quizzed" on this as they were being baptized. This informs pastors how doctrinal preparation for baptismal candidates should be important for churches today.

---

8 Norman, *The Baptist Way*, 142.
9 Ibid., 143.
10 Ibid.

Before I baptize any professing believer, I meet with him or her and have the person share with me their understanding of what it means to trust Christ for salvation and eternal life. I then review the basics of the Christian life, including who Christ is, what He has done, what He is doing, what the cross means, and the resurrection to a victorious triumphant life. I emphasize the need to become a committed disciple (learner, follower) of Jesus Christ.

I have often given the candidate notes or a book about the basics of the Christian life, explaining the meaning of baptism, the Lord's Supper, and church membership. A book I have distributed to new believers is George Sweeting's *How to Begin the Christian Life*, available in paperback. If the church I am serving has a printed constitution and bylaws, I give candidates for baptism a copy.

In preparation for baptism, I tell the candidate to bring an extra set of clothes and a towel. I take the candidate to the baptismal location in the church and rehearse how the baptism will take place. I baptize men one way (hands folded on their chest) and women another way (arms crossed on their chest) in view of where I place my hands. I immerse the men with my hand where their hands are folded and my other hand on their back. For women, I immerse them by placing my right hand on their forehead and my other hand on their back.

If individuals want to hold their nose, I have them hold their own nose with one hand and their arm with the other hand. There are different ways to baptize; irrespective, the best way is to have the person squat down as you baptize him or her. Watch the water level for children and adjust when necessary. I contact the deacon or deacon's wife responsible to assist with the baptism as well as the person assigned to get the water ready for the baptismal service, usually on Sunday morning.

When in the baptismal pool with candidates, I ask, "Do you believe that Jesus Christ is the Son of God?" (Luke 2:11; Acts 8:37-38) and "Have you trusted in Christ as your Lord and Savior?" After their positive confession, I baptize them, saying, "Buried with Christ in baptism, risen to walk in a new life in Him."

The Lord's Supper

Baptists and other evangelicals believe that the Lord's Supper is an ordinance — that which is ordered by Christ. It is not a sacrament administering or dispensing grace, even though Baptists may have employed the term in the past with a different meaning, just as some Protestant churches do today using the term "sacrament."

Norman speaks to the essence of The Lord's Supper: "As the church comes together at the Lord's Table, corporate observance of the supper should promote unity and love among the members of the fellowship. In every way, the encouragement of faith and mission that the ordinances bring serve to strengthen the faith of the church … The ordinances are also timely reminders of what God has done and has yet to do."[11]

Some denominations such as Lutherans, Presbyterians, and Methodists use terms such as **Eucharist** from the Greek word *eucharisteō*, emphasizing the observance as a thanksgiving celebration (Matt. 26:27; 1 Cor. 11:24). **Communion** is another term used to emphasize the fellowship shared among the participants between them and the risen Lord (1 Cor. 10:16-17). **Breaking of Bread** is used in Acts 2:41, 20:7; **the Lord's Table** in 1 Corinthians 10:21.

The observance is reminiscent of the Last Supper Jesus had with the apostles, a Passover meal, in which He gave new meaning to the elements of the bread and the fruit of the vine (Matt. 26:17-30; Mark 14:12-26; Luke 22:7-23). The bread represents the broken body of Christ, and the fruit of the vine represents the blood of the new covenant shed for the

---

11 Norman, *The Baptist Way*, 156.

remission (forgiveness) of sins.

The early church began to observe the Lord's Supper on a regular basis (1 Cor. 11:23). The Apostle Paul broke bread on the first day of the week with the disciples at Troas (Acts 20:7, 11). Guidance for the observance is found in Matthew 26:26-30; Mark 14:22-26; Luke 22:14-20; 1 Corinthians 11:17-34.

- *Elements to be used:* bread and a cup of the fruit of the vine.
- *Procedure:* The observance remembers the night in which Jesus took the bread and the cup and gave new significance to it in terms of His broken body and shed blood. The bread represents His broken body, and the cup represents the new covenant in His blood. Participants are to examine (judge) themselves regarding anything that may stand between them and God and them and another person.

Theological Meaning of the Lord's Supper

The following statements and Scriptures speak to the meaning of the Lord's Supper:

1. A proclamation of the gospel (1 Cor. 11:26).
2. A visual sermon proclaiming the death of Jesus Christ. The bread speaks of His broken body; the fruit of the vine speaks of His shed blood for the sins of the world.
3. The Supper is a symbolic reenactment of His sacrificial death upon the cross, a time to remember the significance of His death until He comes.
4. It is a response to His command: "Do this in remembrance of Me" (Luke 22:19).
5. Participants declare their personal corporate union with Christ as well as their fellowship with one another.
6. It is a time to be reminded of the return of Jesus Christ (1 Cor. 11:26).

Historical Views of the Supper

Roman Catholics in the twelfth century began to use the term "transubstantiation" to suggest that the actual physical body of Christ is present and ingested at the observance called the Mass.

Martin Luther, sometime after 1517, held to a literal, physical presence of the risen Christ found in, with, and under the elements. This view came to be known as "consubstantiation" (even though Luther never used the term), which means that the consecrated bread and wine undergo no change of substance — but the Eucharist is nonetheless the true body and blood of Jesus, in that the elements co-exist with the spiritual body and blood of Christ.

Ulrich Zwingli took issue with Luther between 1525 and 1527, believing that Christ's presence is not found in the elements themselves but in the believing community — thus, the Supper is a memorial commemorating the death of Jesus. This is the view of Baptists and other evangelicals. The elements are visible symbols that reenact the gospel in a visible way. In the Passover meal, all the elements were symbolic reminders.

John Calvin, around 1536, expressed his view that Christ is uniquely present in the Eucharist — not physically, but spiritually, in a dynamic way that has spiritual efficacy or results for the believers.

Who Can Participate in the Ordinance?

Baptists generally believe that this ordinance is to be shared only by believers who have confessed their faith and been baptized. Churches typically observe the ordinance in two ways: **(1) open communion** — it is left up to the participant to partake of it according to their personal faith; **(2) closed communion** — only local church members in good standing with the Lord and each other are invited to participate; visitors are dismissed.

Believers see the ordinance in two different ways: **(1) communal ordinance** — the Lord's Supper could be observed anywhere with a group of believers led by any believer; **(2) church ordinance** — the Lord's Supper is reserved for observance by the church gathered. Norman sees The Lord's Supper as a corporate rite connected to church discipline, as has been practiced historically. He believes there are some exceptions to this for special situations.[12] Most churches only allow ordained ministers and deacons to conduct the Lord's Supper.

A Variety of Ways to Celebrate the Ordinance

Elements to be used: unfermented wine (recommended, even though some Protestants use fermented wine) or unsweetened grape juice, unleavened bread or wafers.

[An interesting fact: Dr. Thomas Bramwell Welch was a British-American dentist and Methodist minister. He pioneered the use of pasteurization as a means of preventing the fermentation of grape juice. He persuaded local churches to adopt this non-alcoholic wine substitute for use in the Lord's Supper, calling it "Dr. Welch's Unfermented Wine." Today it is called Welch's Concord Grape Juice.]

The Lord's Supper may be served in the seats or at the altar area of a church, perhaps placed on a table for individuals to pick up themselves or receive from a deacon, elder, usher, or the pastor. As a chaplain in the military, I served the communion elements at an altar rail for those Christians who desired to kneel to receive the communion elements.

How often should the Lord's Supper be observed? Weekly, monthly, once a quarter, once a year. The Bible only states this guidance: "For as often as you eat this bread and drink this cup, you proclaim the Lord's death till He comes" (1 Cor. 11:26).

---

12 Norman, *The Baptist Way*, 153-55.

Preparation for the Ordinance

When planning to observe the Lord's Supper with the church, I work on a message or meditation about the meaning of the Supper, typically from Matthew 26:26-30, Mark 14:22-26, Luke 22:14-20, or 1 Corinthians 11:17-34 — emphasizing the bread as representative of the broken body of Christ and the fruit of the vine symbolizing the shed blood of Jesus for sin, encouraging the individuals who partake of the elements to examine their lives for any sin not repented of or an unreconciled relationship with a fellow believer.

I would encourage you to get a word from the Lord when sharing a message regarding communion. It does not need to be a long meditation. When I lead the Lord's Supper now, usually before the sermon, I try to relate my remarks on the cross in some way to the message that I will preach or have preached.

The deacon or person responsible for setting up the Lord's Supper needs to be coordinated with. If this is your first time observing the Supper with the church, you will need to coordinate in advance with the deacons how you will conduct the service and the way in which they will distribute the elements. Churches usually have a traditional way of serving communion.

In communion services in churches, I typically have deacons come to the communion table and line up to receive the trays of bread and fruit of the vine. I normally will have a deacon say a prayer at the table before the bread is distributed, then another deacon to say a prayer before the distribution of the fruit of the vine. After the trays are returned and the deacons sit down on the first row, I usually serve them. In some churches, one of the deacons will serve me; in other churches, I just take the elements myself after serving the deacons and proceed with the service.

There are times when I build the whole worship service around the

Lord's Supper, but more often the Lord's Supper is served either before or after preaching the sermon. You may want to purchase a Minister's Manual with suggestions for the Lord's Supper and Baptisms. A good one is *Nelson's Minister's Manual*.

CHAPTER 6

INFANT AND CHILD DEDICATIONS, WEDDINGS, AND FUNERALS

This chapter covers infant and child dedications, weddings, and funerals. At times, Jesus laid His hands upon children, prayed for them, and invoked blessings on their behalf (Matt. 19:13-15; Mark 10:13-16). When children were born in Israel, they were presented in the temple and a sacrifice was offered, a lamb if the couple could provide one; if not able to afford a lamb, they could offer a pair of turtle doves or two young pigeons as a burnt offering and sin offering (Lev. 12:1-8; Luke 2:21-24).

In John 2:1-12, there is an account of a wedding attended by Jesus, His mother, and the disciples. The emphasis is about Jesus turning the water into wine; nothing is mentioned about Him conducting the wedding ceremony. A wedding was a happy occasion of feasting in first-century Galilee and Judea, often lasting a week. It was a high and holy celebration following a one-year period of betrothal in which there was no premarital sex. The wedding night after the ceremony was the time to consummate the marriage. Some of the happiest occasions in my life have been in performing and attending weddings of committed Christian couples. Jesus certainly knew the value of blessing relationships of people regarding marriage.

Jesus once interrupted a funeral procession to raise from death a widow's son (Luke 7:11-17), and He raised Lazarus from the dead four days after he had been buried (John 11:1-44). Jewish funeral processions made their way on the day of death from the family home to the tomb. Members of the immediate family placed the body in the tomb while friends and relatives waited outside. Mourning typically took place for seven days, except for parents. Children mourned their parents for a full year until the time of a secondary burial when the family members returned to the tomb for a ceremony, took the bones of the deceased from their resting place on a shelf or a niche, and placed them in a niche, pit, or ossuary with the person's name on it.

As a pastor, you will have the opportunity to bless and pray for children, perform marriage ceremonies, and conduct funerals and memorial services as a representative of Jesus Christ. These will be extended opportunities for you to share God's Word, offer prayers, and encourage individuals, families, and friends gathered for these occasions. And God will empower you for ministry as you draw upon the spiritual resources available in Christ.

Infant, Baby, Child Dedications

As Christians in the Baptist or independent evangelical tradition, we do not baptize or sprinkle babies. However, pastors typically dedicate babies and children to the Lord in worship services. The precedent goes back to the dedication of Samuel to the Lord (1 Sam. 1:19-28) and the presentation of Jesus in the Temple (Luke 2:22-24). The dedication of the firstborn son was required by Mosaic law (Ex. 13:2, 12-15), and a service in which a sacrifice was made for sons and daughters under the Mosaic law also recognized the end of the days of the mother's purification (Lev. 12:1-8).

The service of dedication is not a christening or a naming service

Infant and Child Dedications, Weddings, and Funerals

of godparents to discharge duties in the event both parents die or are unable to take care of the child. In fact, there is no evidence that these types of dedication services were practiced in the days of the formation of the New Testament church. The child dedication service basically is an alternative to infant baptism practiced by certain Christian denominations regarding infant baptism as a rite/ritual/sacrament. No evidence exists of such infant baptisms/christenings being practiced in the first-century church.

The earliest reference to infant baptism is c. AD 180, referenced by Irenaeus. Three passages by Origen (AD 185-c. 254) mention infant baptism as tradition and customary. In these baptisms, if children could not answer for themselves, their parents or someone else from their family was to answer for them. As early as AD 400, Augustine appeals to the universal practice of infant baptism as proof that the church saw infants born with the stain of original sin and that baptism washed away original sin. The infant and child dedication service has nothing to do with ceremonial cleansing or infant baptism.

The infant/baby/child dedication observance is not for the child but for the parents. The act of dedication does not assure anyone that the child will go to heaven upon death. It simply acknowledges that the parents believe that the child is a gift and an entrustment from the Lord (Ps. 127:3) and that they are committing themselves to raise the child for the Lord in His way (Gen. 18:19; Deut. 6:7, 11:19; Ps. 78:4; Prov. 22:6; 2 Tim. 3:15), in the nurture (instruction, training) and admonition (discipline) of the Lord (Eph. 6:4).

The child dedication service is not for unbelieving parents. I would do a service for a single parent who has custody and wants to raise the child for the Lord. I would not do one for a couple not married where there is no strong evidence of conversion and a godly Christian walk.

I like to meet with the parents in advance to discuss the importance of raising the child for the Lord and to go over how this part of the worship service will be conducted. Typically, I have the parents come forward at a designated point in the worship service and face the congregation. Then I read some appropriate Scripture. I usually ask a litany of questions about the faith of the parents and their commitment to raise the child for Christ. Christian bookstores have pre-printed questions for pastors to use with the parents and church family, or you can draft your own questions.

I ask the congregation to pray for this family and to love this child and family, asking the members to assist in raising the child for Christ within the community of faith. In the service I call the child's name, normally the full name. I usually ask the parents to kneel, and I kneel with them and place my hand on the baby's head and lead in a special prayer for the couple and the child, thanking God for this gift to parents and asking the Lord to guide, provide, and watch over the child during his or her life development. I ask God to seal the commitment of the parents to raise the child for Jesus Christ.

Parents need to remember that this is a voluntary vow made to God, who will hold believers accountable for vows (Deut. 23:21-23, Eccl. 5:4-5). I have always given the parents a small New Testament (blue for boys and pink for girls] with the child's name, my name as the officiating pastor, and the date and place of the dedication service.

Importance of Ministry at Weddings and Funerals

When Jim Henry, pastor emeritus, First Baptist Church, Orlando, Florida, was a young pastor, he once received a good piece of advice from the legendary R.G. Lee, who served for years at Bellevue Baptist Church, Memphis, Tennessee. Dr. Lee told Henry, "Stay on your knees, in the Book, and close to your people." Henry commented that "one of the best ways to stay close to your people is to participate in two of their most important family events — weddings and funerals. Some of the greatest occasions for joy I have known have been at Christ-centered weddings."[1]

Henry continues, "People will forget most of our sermons, but they rarely forget our ministry in those monumental events of their lives." He advocates doing weddings and funerals because "many people who attend these events are not believers or they have drifted from the faith, and their hearts are receptive to eternal things." He wrote, "I always shared the gospel at each wedding and funeral and through the years saw many people saved … Jesus showed up at both weddings and funerals. If they were important for our Lord, they should be important to us as pastors."[2]

Weddings

Weddings conducted by pastors should certainly begin with **premarital counseling** — for me, at least one or two times with the couple, better yet over a longer time such as two months or even longer. During premarital counseling, a good resource is a workbook entitled *Before You Say "I Do": A Marriage Preparation Guide for Couples, Revised and Expanded,* Eugene, OR: Harvest House, 1997 by H. Norman Wright and Wes Roberts. I also recommend the book and video by Gary Chapman on *The 5 Love Languages: The Secret to Love That Lasts,* Chicago: Northfield Publishing, 2015.

For forty years, churches have used *Prepare-Enrich* (see www.prepare-enrich.com), a customized couple assessment completed online identifying a couple's strengths and growth areas. It is one of the most widely used programs for premarital counseling and premarital

---

[1] James W. Bryant and Mac Brunson, *The New Guidebook for Pastors* (Nashville: B&H, 2007), 139.
[2] Ibid.

education. It is also used for marriage counseling, marriage enrichment, and dating couples considering engagement.

In performing marriage vows and ceremonies, I never saw myself as a religious justice of the peace as some pastors were in days gone by in America. When my mother agreed to marry my father on a military pass during World War II, the Methodist pastor of my mother's family was sent for and came to my grandparents' home and performed the wedding vows. My parents lived happily for more than sixty years until my mother died. They did not need a big expensive wedding to have a happy Christian marriage. I don't ever remember hearing a cross word between them.

After some years as an Army chaplain, I decided to put my marriage policy in writing for individuals to read. This should help keep individuals in the church from pressuring you to perform weddings you would not be comfortable performing. I would encourage you to consider writing out your marriage policy and make sure it is available for church members to read before you get involved in wedding planning and ceremonies. A church should also put its wedding policy in writing regarding use of the church facilities, cleaning, wedding coordinators, fees if any, and the like.

Once your counseling is complete and you are satisfied that you can perform the wedding, then you will have to come to terms on the ceremony. Most couples will permit you to do the ceremony your way, perhaps with a few recommendations or modifications. However, some couples will want to write their own vows. You will need to look over these vows, and, if necessary, negotiate with them for the sake of your conscience before God and man. Some modern couples will not like the language of the traditional and modified Episcopal ceremony, as the bride will not want to promise to "obey" her husband. I have substituted the word "respect" or "honor" for "obey."

If the church does not have a wedding coordinator, encourage the couple to find an experienced one (usually a woman) in the community. The exception might be if this is a simple stand-up ceremony with no music or congregation attending, just a small group of family or close friends. The wedding coordinator will handle the details of the wedding so that all you must do is guide the rehearsal of the vows and perform the ceremony. You may or may not want to attend the rehearsal dinner (depending on your schedule), but you should certainly attend the wedding reception after the wedding just as Jesus did at the wedding feast in Cana (John 2).

You will want to get a good wedding manual or develop your own ceremony, observing as much of the tradition as possible, including the giving away of the bride, vows, ring exchanges, lighting of the unity candle, prayers (kneeling or standing), the kiss, and the presentation as husband and wife to the attendees. If you include a message, make it brief, particularly if the bride and groom will be standing. Reading of Scripture and prayers are most appropriate. Review the details — you must not forget anything important. Don't get mixed up like the pastor who said to the man, "Wilt thou take this woman to be thy awful (instead of lawful) wedded wife? What God has joined asunder, let no man put together!" He should have closed by saying, "What God has joined together, let no man put asunder."

As the pastor, you may have to remind the couple of what they are to do and say up there on the platform area. They may be giggly and nervous with knees knocking. Expect anything — even be prepared for someone to faint!

Funerals

Funerals are an occasion to minister to people and their families. Customs regarding funerals differ according to cultures, communities, and local traditions. It might be a good idea to attend a funeral in your new community before conducting a funeral.

Once you have given pastoral care at the time of death, you will need to meet with the widow or widower and family about funeral arrangements. You will discuss with them the time and place of the funeral service and burial, Scriptures to be read, whether eulogies will be given and by whom, music, the message, and other considerations, such as coordination with military representatives for a veteran or organizational representatives who want to be involved.

Afterward, coordinate with the funeral home. You may or may not be required to do a bulletin or give input for the bulletin if there will be one. It will be the responsibility of the funeral director to prepare an obituary for the newspaper. You may want to meet with the family after they have made the arrangements at the funeral home.

You will then have to plan the funeral service. Remember: The funeral service is to help bring a sense of closure to the family. The service is not for you or for the church — it is for the family, even though the church members and friends will be ministered to in the funeral service.

Learn as much as you can about the deceased, his or her story (history), spiritual orientation, faith, whether the person had favorite Bible verses, hymns, poetry, or songs. It would be helpful to know what his or her interests were — you may use this in the sermon or find something in the Bible for your message that relates. Above all, make the funeral personal and not a canned kind of service, like some I have been to when the minister read the entire service from a funeral manual.

If you know, suspect, or learn that the individual was not a faithful Christian, it is not a good idea to say, suggest, or imply that the deceased went out into a Christ-less eternity. Your job is to bring comfort to the family, remembering that God is keeping the accurate record book on an individual's destiny.

Infant and Child Dedications, Weddings, and Funerals

Find out if someone in the family or friends wants to bring a eulogy, or if the family just wants you to read an obituary, perhaps adding some details you have learned about the individual. Find out if members of the family or friends want to say something. No more than two or three should speak, and they should be given a time limit (several minutes).

Find out if representatives of fraternal organizations will participate. Find out if the deceased was a veteran of the armed forces and if there will be military honors at the interment (burial). If so, you will need to coordinate with the funeral director and/or the honor guard or organizational leader. Have prearranged signals for smooth coordination at the graveside service.

Be sure to pray with the family when you visit and assure them that you will do your best to honor the deceased loved one. Find some positive things to say about the individual or emphasize some strong qualities. You should not try to preach someone into heaven if there is doubt about their spiritual condition. Above all, don't say anything derogatory. With God's help, strive to comfort the family!

If there is a procession, you will typically lead it (whether it is walking up to the church from the funeral cars or walking up to the gravesite). If there is no procession to the church or chapel, you will just walk up to the podium before the family is seated in the church or chapel and have the congregation stand until the family is in their seats. Fewer and fewer funeral services are being conducted at churches these days. It is more common for the funeral to be held at the mortuary chapel, thereafter the attendees will caravan from the mortuary to the cemetery for the burial.

If you have not already done so, you will need to purchase one or two good funeral manuals, usually available at a Christian bookstore or online. I have always prepared every funeral service uniquely and as "individually" as I could. "Canned" funeral services are not good. As a military chaplain and interim pastor, I had to do funeral and memorial services on short notice for people I did not know. Even if you do not know the person or family, plan to make a visit before the service and sit down with the survivor(s), getting to know as much as you can about the person, assuring the family you will give them your best.

Always be early to the church or funeral home. Know the names of the close family members and how to pronounce them properly (check this out in advance), even if you must write the names down on paper phonetically and put the list in your Bible. Sometimes nervousness makes you forget.

You must be "appropriate" in a funeral service. Typically, forty-five minutes to an hour is long enough, unless the family asks for it to be longer or shorter. If the individual is a community leader or dignitary, then a more extended service will be planned. Funeral services for very well-known national or community leaders may last as long as two hours. However, this will be very rare.

Remember to have the congregation stand as the family arrives and departs. If a funeral entourage arrives with the family at the church, meet them as they get out of the vehicles or at the front door of the church if the funeral director will bring them to the front of the church for seating.

Open or closed casket or cremation will be decided in advance. More and more, people are bringing pictures of the departed to the mortuary or church or have a video presentation of the person's life on a screen to view before the service begins or even during the service. A typical funeral service will usually have a greeting (welcome), Old and New Testament readings, prayers, eulogy or reading of the obituary, music (congregational hymns and/or solos). Sometimes family members may want to read a poem or letter. Make sure it is appropriate and in good taste — most of the time it will be.

Infant and Child Dedications, Weddings, and Funerals 73

As the pastor or chaplain, you will usually bring a short message. Make it appropriate and speak kindly and lovingly of the deceased. If you are led to give an invitation to trust Christ, I would not invite people to come forward or pressure them to raise their hands. It is not a good idea to say things like, "If you want to see this person again, you better repent of your sins and trust Jesus." Sometimes the most immediate member of the deceased will ask you to give an invitation for attendees to trust Christ or the departed one may have asked you before death to give an invitation. Be wise about invitations in funeral services.

Graveside Services and Interment

You can usually drive your own car or ride with the funeral director to the cemetery. The pastor (chaplain or minister) is typically lined up at the front of the procession of cars. If the funeral coach is not leading the caravan and you are going to have to lead the procession, you better know the exact location of the cemetery and how to get there. The advantage of driving your own car is that you can leave and get on to the next place after the service. It is better to have a dark automobile if you will use your own vehicle in the procession.

For both the funeral and graveside service, my recommendation is that you, unless you are a military chaplain, will need a black suit, white shirt, with a conservative necktie, black shoes, and socks. You would be wise to invest in a black overcoat and raincoat for outdoor services in inclement weather. Today many men do not attend funeral services in suit and tie; casual seems to be what is popular, but a suit is more appropriate for the occasion.

When you arrive at the graveside, go to the funeral coach with the corpse and stand there respectfully while the casket is unloaded. Then you and the director will usually proceed to the gravesite. Position yourself at the head of the deceased (in the past it was always to the east) and face the next-of-kin who are always on the front row.

Read some appropriate Scriptures, make a few comments, recite or read a committal of the body back to the earth from which it came, and close in prayer. If the funeral service is a graveside-only service, you will want to elongate it in coordination with the family's wishes and the funeral director. The general rule at graveside services is to be brief but don't rush. I remember being at a graveside service when the pastor made it so brief and quick that the widow said out loud, "Is that all?" Again, if there is only a graveside service, you will include elements of the funeral service at the gravesite.

Find out what is meaningful for the family. After the benediction, you will usually speak to the members of the immediate family, especially those on the first row (usually it is too confined to go into the second row) with words of comfort. Then position yourself nearby and let the funeral director take charge. Always have some breath mints when you will be providing pastoral care in close proximity to people. If there are military honors, find out about the folding and presentation of the flag and the playing of "Taps." Coordinate a signal for the officer in charge of the military honor guard. "Taps" may conclude the service, or you could do a benediction after "Taps."

CHAPTER 7

THE PASTOR'S PRAYER AND HOME LIFE

In Acts 6:1-7, we read how the church in Jerusalem selected seven wise and Spirit-filled men to distribute the food among the needy when there was an issue raised by the Hellenistic Jews against the Hebraic Jews that their widows were being neglected in the daily food distribution. The apostles gave some serious consideration to what they were doing each day and concluded they needed help with serving the tables. Apparently, this effort was causing them to neglect prayer and the ministry of the Word of God, which should have been a priority in their spiritual leadership of the church.

This is so typical of pastors today who are servants of God that may try to do everything themselves simply because they can and are willing. The apostles had contributed to their own problem because they were trying to do too much. Pastors can get so involved in secondary ministry tasks that they fail to spend adequate time in prayer and study of God's Word, and it will impact the church since a church will not rise any higher spiritually than its leadership.

Serving tables is not menial work, because every ministry task in the church is important. But the fact of the matter is that the apostles were doing jobs that others could have done just as well. As a pastor of churches with less than 200 on the roll, I had the view that every member of the church should have a job in the church — and it was my responsibility to get people involved in some type of body life ministry in the church. This will give pastors the time they need to daily feed themselves the Word of God and have a significant prayer life. Dr. Jimmy Draper, a pastor for many years before he became president of Lifeway Christian Resources, said when he pastored churches with a staff, he would arrive at the church around 6:00 a.m. and have several hours of Bible study and prayer before the church staff arrived.

Jesus knew the Twelve needed to know about prayer and the ministry of the Word. He taught them about prayer and modeled it before them. He taught them by example, with parables, through encounters with people, and in private after speaking to crowds with spiritual lessons they could remember and teach to others themselves. And Jesus knew the apostles needed rest, times of retreat, and recuperation from their preaching and ministry assignments, telling them on one occasion to "Come aside by yourselves to a deserted place and rest a while" (Mark 6:31).

Some of His apostles and disciples had believing wives who traveled with them in ministry, which necessitated income to provide for them (1 Cor. 9:5). Philip the evangelist, for example, had four daughters living with him in Caesarea (Acts 21:8-9). He surely knew about family life. The early church held a high standard for pastors to be men of the Word, prayer, and to lead and provide for their families well (1 Tim. 5:8). Let us follow Christ with all our hearts in doing these things.

The Pastor's Home

One of the qualifications for the pastor (overseer, elder) is that he "rules [manages, NASB, NIV] his own house well [completely, HCSB], having his children in submission with all reverence (for if a man does not know how to rule his own house, how will he take care of the church of God?)" (1 Tim. 3:4-5) and "having faithful children not accused of dissipation or insubordination [being wild and disobedient, NIV]" (Tit. 1:6). How a pastor protects, guides, and provides for his family will be a good indication of how he will lead Christ's church. One of the great challenges of being a pastor is that people are constantly watching him and his family; he, his wife, and their children are always on display before the congregation in the church and community. This has been called the fishbowl of ministry.

Paul knew that a pastor is not going to lead a church any better than he leads his own home. For that reason, having a godly life before your wife and children must be a priority in pastoral ministry. One of the greatest compliments I ever heard about Billy Graham was what Franklin Graham said at his father's funeral: "The Billy Graham that the world saw on television, the Billy Graham that the world saw in big stadiums, was the same Billy Graham we saw at home. There weren't two Billy Grahams."[1] Pastor Greg Laurie, who served on the board of directors of the Billy Graham organization for twenty-five years and spent much time with him, said the same thing in his book *Billy Graham: The Man I Knew*: "There were not two Billy Grahams. He was the same man in private that he was in public."

The pastor's relationship with his family is key and essential to a good pastorate. John Bisagno writes, "The pastor and his family are subject to the same trials and temptations as other families. Being in the ministry is no guarantee of rearing a perfect family … There is, however, something special about a pastor with a good family. The love and care he receives from them and the nurture he gives to them can be

---

1 Franklin Graham: "There Weren't Two Billy Grahams," accessed online 12 July 2021, https://www.wfae.org/local-news/2018-03-02/franklin-graham-there-weren't-two-billy-grahams.

important factors in his spiritual development as an under-shepherd to the family of God ... And, of course, there is enhanced credibility when a happily married pastor speaks on matters of marriage and family life."[2] Bisagno makes a good point when he says, "Dear pastor, be exceedingly clear with your family and your congregation that neither your spouse nor your children must ever feel any pressure to do or to be anything for any other reason than their love for the Lord Jesus."[3]

Some Bible Verses About the Home for Pastors

Despite some mistakes in ministry, the wisest thing I did through the years was to ask the Lord to help me love my wife as Christ loved the church and gave Himself for it (Eph. 5:25) and to raise our children for the Lord as Joshua said when speaking to Israel, "But as for me and my house, we will serve the Lord" (Josh. 24:15). Here are some verses from the Scriptures guiding me as a pastor through the years with my assignment from the Lord:

Deuteronomy 6:4-9: "Hear, O Israel: The Lord our God, the Lord *is* one! You shall love the Lord your God with all your heart, with all your soul, and with all your strength. And these words which I command you today shall be in your heart. You shall teach them diligently to your children and shall talk of them when you sit in your house, when you walk by the way, when you lie down, and when you rise up. You shall bind them as a sign on your hand, and they shall be as frontlets between your eyes. You shall write them on the doorposts of your house and on your gates."

Proverbs 13:24: "He who spares his rod hates his son, but he who

---

2 John Bisagno, *Pastor's Handbook* (Nashville: B&H Publishing Group, 2011), 61.
3 Ibid.

loves him disciplines him promptly."

Proverbs 22:6: "Train up a child in the way he should go, and when he is old he will not depart from it."

Proverbs 23:13-14: "Do not withhold correction from a child, for *if* you beat him with a rod, he will not die. You shall beat him with a rod and deliver his soul from hell.

Proverbs 29:15: "The rod and rebuke give wisdom, but a child left *to himself* brings shame to his mother."

Ephesians 6:4: "And you, fathers, do not provoke your children to wrath, but bring them up in the training and admonition [instruction] of the Lord."

Colossians 3:21: "Fathers, do not provoke your children, lest they become discouraged."

Don't think for one minute that I was a cruel abuser of our children with corporal punishment and family discipline. The rod simply meant *a neutral object* and not my hand or foot. My wife and I learned this in the first year of our marriage at a marriage seminar. The rod could be anything from a book, Bible, switch, paddle, or belt. And I never spanked them hard as children; usually one whack for them to know I would not tolerate blatant disobedience or disrespect.

And I used teachable moments to quote the Bible and its truth in the course of daily living and situations that came up. My wife and I are so grateful that our children love the Lord, married committed Christians, are active in their churches, and are raising their children for the Lord. Yes, I made mistakes and went overboard sometimes with suspension of privileges, but the Lord would convict me, and I would reduce the original sentence to something reasonable and ask the child to forgive their impulsive father. I am so grateful for a godly Christian wife and mother of our children who saw the extreme importance of our children's emotional and physical needs being met, as well as moral and spiritual guidance. When the children were little, my wife read Bible stories to them from a red hardcover book entitled *The Picture Bible*, still in print.

Tips on the Challenges of Leading the Home as a Pastor

Here are some things I have learned through the years (often from my wife and godly Christians) about leading our home as a husband, father, and pastor:

1. The husband and wife must love and respect each other and agree about basic Christian teachings and values from the Bible.
2. The husband and wife need some quality time together each week (date nights recommended), as well as time with the entire family (vacations if affordable to do fun things).
3. Prayer needs to be prominent in the home at meals, devotional times, bedtime with the young children, and whenever there is a crisis affecting the family or one of the members of the family
4. Parents should be united on how to discipline the children.
5. Parents should agree about the Christian education of the children.
6. Parents need to manage the finances of the home wisely, keeping in mind biblical teachings regarding giving, spending, saving, investing, conserving, and stewardship in general. It is never too early to teach the children biblical principles about money. I taught our children to tithe a tenth of every gift they received and what money they earned. As adults they have prospered financially.
7. Fathers and mothers should find ways to spend time with the children and support them in study, extracurricular activities,

and their work around the home. Put the children's activities on your calendar and in your day-planner. Be there for their programs, activities, and events. I can see our sons and daughter looking up into the stands to see where Dad and Mom were sitting and would be cheering for their team in sporting events. As a pastor, I once showed up late to a tennis match our daughter was playing, and I started cheering loudly like I was at a football game when our sons were playing. People began to shush me to get me to be quiet — I didn't know the spectator rules of tennis matches.

The Pastor's Prayer Life

The pastor needs to be like Jesus in that He was a "man of prayer." The pastor must have a prayer closet (a place) where he can secretly meet God for prayer about his own life, his family, the church, and others. Jesus said, "But when you pray, go into your room [closet (KJV), inner room (NASB)], and when you have shut your door, pray to your Father who is in the secret place, and your Father who sees in secret will reward you openly" (Matt. 6:6). In other words, when you pray, things will happen as God hears and answers your prayers in accord with His divine will, purposes, and your faith. A senior pastor I respected greatly, now with the Lord, once told me how he built a prayer closet in his home and spent the first hour of his day there (when not traveling) before going to the church. He found many of the issues he was concerned about were solved when he arrived at his church office.

When Jesus went into the Garden of Gethsemane to pray, He asked the disciples to pray that they not enter temptation (Luke 22:40), but when He returned to them, they had fallen asleep. Jesus said to Peter, "What! Could you not watch with Me one hour?" (Matt. 26:46; Mark 14:37); "Why do you sleep? Rise and pray, lest you enter into temptation"

(Luke 22:46). I have read how effective former pastors like Ronnie Floyd point to this verse and advise that pastors spend at least an hour a day in prayer. John Bisagno, in a lecture to students I taught at the seminary in 2005, recommended an hour a day, seven days a week, for pastors to be on their knees before God in prayer in the early morning hours. He wrote, "When you spend that early morning time in prayer, you will have fewer problems and fewer obstacles. When you get to the problems you fear and the situations you dread, you will often find God has already been there before you, and your day is easier and shorter."[4] Bisagno quotes Isaiah 65:24 in this regard: "Even before they call, I will answer."

James Rosscup recommends two passages by Jesus and Paul as strategic in merging the Word of God and prayer in pastoral ministry:[5]

(1) John 15:7-8: "If you abide in Me, and My words abide in you, you will ask what you desire, and it shall be done for you. By this My Father is glorified, that you bear much fruit; so you will be My disciples." Rosscup comments, "Abiding is at the heart of the Christian life according to the greatest of all shepherds."[6] He goes on to say abiding is praying in ways God's Word prescribes and this kind of praying results in a life of glorification, multiplication, and authentication."[7] I once visited the Moody Church in Chicago on a Wednesday night and one of the associate pastors brought a lesson on praying Scripture back to God, reminding the Lord what He has said in His Word and formulating our prayers accordingly.

(2) Ephesians 6:10-20: "Finally, my brethren, be strong in the

---

4 Bisagno, *Pastor's Handbook*, 101.
5 James E. Rosscup, "The Pastor's Prayer Life — The Personal Side" in *Pastoral Ministry: How to Shepherd Biblically*, John Macarthur and The Master's Seminary Faculty (Nashville: Thomas Nelson Publishers, 2005), 131-43.
6 Ibid., 131.
7 Ibid., 132-33.

Lord and in the power of His might. Put on the whole armor of God, that you may be able to stand against the wiles of the devil. For we do not wrestle against flesh and blood, but against principalities, against powers, against the rulers of the darkness of this age, against spiritual hosts of wickedness in the heavenly places. Therefore, take up the whole armor of God, that you may be able to withstand in the evil day, and have done all, to stand. Stand therefore, having girded your waist with truth, having put on the breastplate of righteousness, and having shod your feet with the preparation of the gospel of peace; above all, taking the shield of faith with which you will be able to quench all the fiery darts of the wicked one. And take the helmet of salvation, and the sword of the Spirit, which is the word of God; praying always with all prayer and supplication in the Spirit, being watchful to this end with all perseverance and supplication for all the saints — and for me, that utterance may be given to me, that I may open my mouth boldly to make known the mystery of the gospel, for which I am an ambassador in chains; that in it I may speak boldly, as I ought to speak." Rosscup points out there is power in the armor that pastors have access to in their prayer life: "Christians secure that power by appropriating weaponry God has made available."[8] Prayer is empowered by the parts of the armor: truth, peace, righteousness, faith, salvation, and the Word of God.

As referred to several times before, in the early Jerusalem church, the Christians selected spiritually committed men to take care of the distribution of the food to the widows, while the apostles said, "But we will give ourselves continually to prayer and to the ministry of the Word" (Acts 6:4). When the apostles gave themselves to prayer and the ministry of the Word, "by their example they evidenced that the two

best ways of knowing and yielding to the mind of God are prayer and

---

8 Rosscup, *Pastoral Ministry*, 148.

a commitment to reading, obeying, and teaching God's Word without rationalization or reservation. Prayer was, and is, a major key."[9]

The pastor must not only pray himself, but he must lead the corporate body to pray (often at a midweek prayer service) and facilitate small-group prayer meetings during the week. Unfortunately, at many churches the midweek prayer meeting becomes a Bible study with a little prayer thrown in after a prayer list is distributed, gathered, or read. An effective pastor I know started the week with an early-morning men's prayer meeting. Women may schedule prayer meetings when it is convenient. Church staff meetings are also a good time for prayer with leaders in ministry.

When I was in seminary in the 1970s, for a number of months I was an all-night security guard at a large evangelical church that had a twenty-four-hour prayer room and ministry where church members signed up for blocks of time to come and pray. My job was to make sure those coming for prayer during their shift could safely get into the church and back to their cars. Men came after dark. There was a logbook for the prayer requests and answers to be written in, and a phone for people to call in prayer requests and speak with the person assigned to be in the prayer room.

---

9 Rosscup, *Pastoral Ministry*, 148.

CHAPTER 8

JESUS AND SHEPHERDING CARE

Shortly after I surrendered to the lordship of Christ at twenty-one years of age, I was drawn to a deacon and Sunday School teacher who worked in my father's grocery store. While working together, we would talk about the Bible most every day, and he would encourage me to memorize certain passages from the Scriptures he had memorized. One of those passages has stayed with me to this day as a focus for pastoral and chaplaincy ministry. The passage does not endorse a social gospel only, but it is a viable component of the whole gospel of Jesus — who cared for the soul, the body, the mind, the emotions, the past, the present, the future, and the entire life of the people He ministered to. The passage is Matthew 25:31-46:

> *When the Son of Man comes in His glory, and all the holy angels with Him, then He will sit on the throne of His glory. All the nations will be gathered before Him, and He will separate them one from another, as a shepherd divides his sheep from the goats. And He will set the sheep on His right hand, but the goats on the left. Then the King will say to those on His right hand, "Come, you blessed of My Father, inherit the kingdom prepared for you from the foundation of the world: for I was hungry and you gave Me food; I was thirsty and you gave Me drink; I was a stranger*

and you took Me in; I was naked and you clothed Me; I was sick and you visited Me; I was in prison and you came to Me." Then the righteous will answer Him, saying, "Lord, when did we see You hungry and feed You, or thirsty and give You drink? When did we see You a stranger and take You in, or naked and clothe You? Or when did we see You sick, or in prison, and come to You?" And the King will answer and say to them, "Assuredly, I say to you, inasmuch as you did it to one of the least of these My brethren, you did it to Me." Then He will also say to those on the left hand, "Depart from Me, you cursed, into the everlasting fire prepared for the devil and his angels: for I was hungry and you gave Me no food; I was thirsty and you gave Me no drink; I was a stranger and you did not take Me in, naked and you did not clothe Me, sick and in prison and you did not visit Me." Then they also will answer Him, saying, "Lord, when did we see You hungry or thirsty or a stranger or naked or sick or in prison, and did not minister to You?" Then He will answer them, saying, "Assuredly, I say to you, inasmuch as you did not do it to one of the least of these, you did not do it to Me." And these will go away into everlasting punishment, but the righteous into eternal life.

What this passage is teaching is that our ministry as Christian leaders must be more than preaching, teaching, and attending gatherings of the church; we must reach out to provide loving care to those who are hungry, thirsty, homeless, without adequate clothing, sick and in prison needing a visit from a caring Christian. Christ-centered ministry not only is concerned about the conversion of the soul but compassionate care of the whole person demonstrated as many ways as possible.

The apostles of Jesus carried a money bag out of which they could give funds to those in need, as well as provide for themselves as they traveled. Some people have the idea that pastors simply prepare sermons to preach on Sunday and do little else but attend occasional meetings. Derek Prime and Alistair Begg speak to such a view: "What is done in public on a Sunday is like the tip of an iceberg. Behind all true preaching by shepherds and teachers there are hours of study and preparation linked with deep involvement in people's lives — an involvement in which there are no regular 'working hours.' Pastoral care is at one and the same time the most demanding and rewarding task there can be."[1] However, the larger the church, the more challenging it is to do high quality pastoral care ministry.

If God has called you to prepare for and to enter pastoral ministry, you have a high calling to represent Christ to lost and hurting people. The Apostle Paul understood his calling to ministry when he wrote introductions in letters to churches such as this one to the Romans: "Paul, a bondservant of Jesus Christ, called to be an apostle, separated to the gospel of God" (Rom. 1:1). In 2 Corinthians 4:5, Paul spoke of himself and his associates in ministry as "your bondservants for Jesus's sake." A bondservant did the will of his master and cared for him and his family as devoutly as possible.

Shepherding Is Pastoral Care

Shepherding people of the church is pastoral care, understood by Derek Prime and Alistair Begg as "the practical, individual, and spiritual care of Christ's people as His lambs and sheep."[2] Pastoral care of the congregation accompanies the preaching, teaching, and administrative duties of a pastor. The Roman Catholic Bishop Gregory the Great

---

1 Derek Prime and Alistair Begg, *On Being a Pastor: Understanding Our Calling and Work* (Chicago: Moody, 2004), 150.
2 Ibid.

(c. 540-604) wrote that "the care of souls is the art of arts."[3] He makes the point that not everyone should be a pastor. Students interested in the pastorate should consider taking an in-depth course in pastoral care or spend time being mentored by an experienced pastor. I am grateful to God for the godly and wise mentors in pastoral care ministry I learned from in my earliest years serving the Lord in churches and chapel congregations.

Carl Volz, Lutheran scholar, defines pastoral care as meaning "the concern for the spiritual and physical welfare of individual Christians on a personal and intimate level, or in contemporary parlance, on a one-to-one basis."[4] Volz says pastors must give "devoted time to the care of individuals in their various spiritual and emotional crises."[5]

Pastoral care is church soul care, an integral function of biblical shepherding. Compassionate care was very much a part of the mission of Jesus as the Messiah (Luke 4:18-19), care that can been seen in the actions of the Good Samaritan (Luke 10:33-35). Pastoral care can be understood as what God in Christ does for others through ministers enabled by the work of the Holy Spirit; an expression of the gospel delivered to people through our union with Christ; and exists in the church as the communication of the Word of God to individuals.

Pastoral Care as Soul Care

Soul care is a comprehensive concept to describe the work of the spiritual care of the souls entrusted to a pastor. The practice comes from the ancient Latin *cura animarum*, meaning "care of souls" or the

---

3 St. Gregory the Great, *The Book of Pastoral Rule*, trans. George E. Demacopoulos (Crestwood, NY: St. Vladimir's Seminary Press, 2007), 29.
4 Carl Volz, *Pastoral Life and Practice in the Early Church* (Minneapolis: Augsburg, 1990), 139.
5 Ibid.

emotional, social, physical, and spiritual support of individuals. We call this pastoral care today or spiritual shepherding.

Hebrews 13:17 reminds us that pastors will give account before God regarding their sphere of shepherding ministry: "Obey those who rule over you, and be submissive, for they watch out for your souls, as those who must give account."

Soul care is much more than having encouraging words for the saints. It is also convincing [correcting], reproving [rebuking], and exhorting [urging] with all longsuffering and doctrine [teaching] (2 Tim. 4:2), much of which is done by one-on-one admonitions, counseling, and care. Ezekiel 33:7-9 is a passage that speaks to soul care, in the sense of watchmen warning those who are living wickedly to repent of their sinful activities.

Thomas Oden says, "The soul is that by which we most deeply feel, know, and will, and by which the body is animated. The soul lives out of God, and in life transcends this mortal sphere ... It is to the soul that the truth is made known."[6] Care of souls is the care of the inner life of persons that pastors give individuals on behalf of God, who is the Chief Shepherd of Care, remembering how "God cares for you" (1 Pet. 5:7).

Five Functions of Pastoral Care

Some years ago, pastoral care was described in four functions by William A. Clebsch and Charles R. Jaekle in *Pastoral Care in Historical Perspective* (1964). Howard Clinebell added a fifth function in *Basic Types of Pastoral Care & Counseling* (1964, 1984).

Healing is "a pastoral function that aims to overcome some impairment by restoring the person to wholeness and by leading him or

---

6 Thomas Oden, *Pastoral Theology: Essentials of Ministry* (San Francisco: Harper, 1989), 86.

her to advance beyond their previous condition."[7] We see healing in the ministry of Jesus and the apostles (Matt. 4:23-24; 10:1, 8; Luke 10:9). All of the healings Jesus did were not recorded (John 20:30). Elders in churches were involved in healing (James 5:14-16). Paul wrote that sin prevents healing and may lead to sickness and death (1 Cor. 11:27-32). Healings are a spiritual gift given to believers in the Body of Christ (1 Cor. 12:9). Some Christians, pastors, and professors believe there is healing in the atonement of Christ as prophesied in Isa. 53:4 (see Matt. 8:16-17). Peter spoke of spiritual healing in the work of Jesus on the cross (1 Pet. 2:24).

Harold Sala writes that healing takes place in four ways:

miraculous healing — instantaneously in answer to prayer (Matt. 17:14-21); Mark 9:14-29)

natural or integrative healing — through the hands of skilled physicians in whom God works (Matt. 9:12)

delayed healing — sometimes healing is delayed due to God's redemptive purposes (2 Cor. 12:8-10)

final or ultimate healing — when God calls a believer to heaven at death (Ps. 116:15; Phil. 1:20-23).[8]

---

7 Howard Clinebell, *Basic Types of Pastoral Care & Counseling* (Nashville: Abingdon, 1984), 42, adopted from William A. Clebsch and Charles R. Jaekle, *Pastoral Care in Historical Perspective* (Northvale, NJ: Jason Aronson Inc., 1975, 1983).

8 Harold Sala, *What You Need to Know About Healing: A Physical and Spiritual Guide* (Nashville: B&H Publishing, 2013). When I had a heart attack while preaching too victoriously on "If the Son Sets You Free" during a Fourth of July worship service in 2013, I read the opening chapters of Sala's book while hospitalized and not able to sleep, waiting for a catheterization the next morning. Providentially, I had bought the book the day before and it was in my briefcase. I was led to pray, "Lord, I know you can heal me miraculously, and I would like to ask you to do that if it would be within your will and for your glory, but if you do not want to do it, I am going to trust you anyway." This prayer gave me perfect peace and I was able to sleep until awakened for the procedure. The cardiologist reported at the end of the procedure: "No blockage and no damage," and I was released from the hospital to return to teaching at Dallas Baptist University.

Sustaining is "a pastoral function that helps a hurting person to endure and to transcend a circumstance in which restoration to his former condition or recuperation from his malady is either impossible or so remote as to seem improbable."[9] Pastors will minister to people with disabilities, injuries, and discouragements about their situation and status in life. Here, the pastor needs to be an encourager out of the spiritual gift to exhort from the Greek word παρακλήσει or *paraklēsei* (Rom. 12:8). Pastors may encourage believers in preaching, teaching, counseling, and visiting. Supportive caring and counseling, crisis counseling, bereavement ministry, and counseling are ways pastoral care is given to sustain a person.

Barnabas was a great example of an encourager (Acts 4:36). Other good verses on encouragement as sustaining are 1 Thessalonians 5:11: "Therefore comfort each other and edify one another, just as you also are doing"; and Hebrews 3:13: "But exhort one another daily, while it is called 'Today,' lest any of you be hardened through the deceitfulness of sin."

Guiding is a pastoral function of "assisting perplexed persons to make confident choices between alternative courses of thought and action when such choices are viewed as affecting the present and future state of the soul."[10] A good shepherd like the Lord guides the sheep of the flock to the green pastures and the still waters (Ps. 23:2-3). God's flock needs spiritual, moral, and theological leadership and guidance.

The pastor must lead God's people in the path of righteousness (Ps. 23:3) and sound doctrine (Tit. 2:1), going before the people in spiritual formation, spiritual warfare, understanding the Word of God, and Christian service and care. Jesus is the Good Shepherd who led sheep willing to follow Him (John 10:1-16, 26-27). He guided His sheep by

---

9 Clinebell, *Basic Types of Pastoral Care & Counseling*, 42.
10 Ibid.

the Word of God and by His life as an example of a spiritual shepherd.

The people of the church are making decisions every day, and they need guidance from the Holy Scriptures that are profitable for **doctrine** [what to believe], for **reproof** [what not to believe], for **correction** [what not to do], for **instruction in righteousness** [what to do] according to 2 Timothy 3:15-17. As the Spirit-filled and wise pastor preaches, teaches, leads, and counsels from the Word of God, people will have the resources to make good decisions and be thoroughly equipped for every good work.

Reconciling is a pastoral function that "seeks to reestablish broken relationships between man and fellow man and between man and God."[11] A key passage is Matthew 5:23-24, which speaks to people needing to be reconciled to each other. Jesus did not always solve every dispute among people. See Luke 12:13-21; He used the occasion to teach about covetousness.

Jesus advocated settling conflicts and differences before worship (Matt. 5:34, 24) or before going to court over a matter (Matt. 5:25-26; Luke 12:57-59), as well as in the context of relationships between people in the church (Matt. 18:15-17). Pastors will be consulted about conflicts in the lives of people in the church. Two excellent books on resolving conflict according to the Scriptures in personal lives and in churches are: Ken Sande's *The Peace Maker: A Biblical Guide to Resolving Personal Conflict* and Jim Van Yperen's *Making Peace: A Guide to Overcoming Church Conflict*.

Regarding conflict resolution, Ken Sande, in his book, shares "Four G's" about conflict resolution and peacemaking:

Glorify God (1 Cor. 10:31) — How can I please and honor God in this situation?

Get the log out of your eye (Matt. 7:5) — How can I show Jesus's

---

11 Clinebell, *Basic Types of Pastoral Care & Counseling*, 42.

work in me by taking responsibility for my contribution to this conflict?

Gently restore (Gal. 6:1) — How can I lovingly serve others by helping them take responsibility for their contribution to this conflict?

Go and be reconciled (Matt. 5:25) — How can I demonstrate the forgiveness of God and encourage a reasonable solution to this conflict?[12]

Jim Van Yperen believes all church conflict is always about leadership and says the way leaders respond to conflict determines if, when, and how the conflict is resolved. He advocates a church embodying a sense of biblical community and a way of life shaped by the Cross of Christ. He understands conflict resolution in churches from Scripture in three ways:

- **Church conflict is always theological, never merely interpersonal.**
- **All church conflict is always about leadership, character, and community.**
- **The lordship of Jesus Christ, not method, should be the object and subject of our search for answers about conflict in the church.**[13]

Nurturing is a pastoral function with the aim "to enable people to develop their God-given potentialities, through the life journey with all its valleys, peaks, and plateaus. In traditional theological language, this process of growth has been called *sanctification*."[14] It is the training of new members in the Christian life (Matt. 28:20; John 21:15-17). This is an important task of all spiritual leaders in the church: to equip the

---

12 Ken Sande, *The Peace Maker: A Biblical Guide to Resolving Personal Conflict*, rev. ed (Grand Rapids: Baker Books, 1991, 1997, 2004), 12-13.
13 Jim Van Yperen, *Making Peace: A Guide to Overcoming Church Conflict* (Chicago: Moody, 2002). 14, 24-25.
14 Clinebell, *Basic Types of Pastoral Care & Counseling*, 43.

saints for Christian living and ministry (Eph. 4:11-16).

New Christians need the milk of the Word (1 Cor. 3:2; 1 Pet. 2:2) and then they will progress to the meat of the Word of God (Heb. 5:12-14) so they may grow strong in the grace and knowledge of Christ (2 Pet. 5:18).

New Christians need to know and practice certain truths as new disciples of Jesus:

1. The doctrine of Christ (2 John 9), the doctrine of the apostles (Acts 2:42), and sound doctrine (Tit. 2:1)
2. The basis of assurance (2 Tim. 1:12; 1 John 5:13) taught by John in 1 John 1:1-5:12
3. Keeping short accounts with God by confessing and repenting of sin (1 John 1:5-10; James 5:15-16)
4. Studying the Word of God (2 Tim. 2:15, 3:15-17)
5. Prayer (Matt. 6:5-15; Luke 11:1-13; 1 Thess. 5:17; 1 Tim. 2:1-7)
6. Sharing the good news of Jesus (Acts 1:8; Mark 16:15; Rom. 1:15-17, 10:9-13)
7. Worship (Luke 4:16; John 4:23-24; Heb. 10:15)
8. Fellowship with other believers (Acts 2:46; 1 John 1:3)
9. Giving to support the work of the church, the needs of the poor, and advancing the gospel where it has not been preached (Matt. 23:23; 1 Cor. 16:1-2; 2 Cor. 8:18-24, 9:1-15)
10. Loving one another (John 13:34-35; Rom. 13:8; 1 John 3:11, 18; 4:12, 13; 1 Pet. 4:8) and forgiving one another (Eph. 4:32; Col. 3:13)

How Pastoral Care Is Delivered

Pastoral care may be delivered in a variety of ways in the context of ministry:

Preaching the Word — Your messages can include pastoral care themes and you can do pastoral care ministry from the pulpit. But don't use people you have counseled as illustrations in your sermons.

Praying for people — You will have many opportunities to pray for people in the pulpit, when in private counseling sessions, and when you are visiting with them. Growing up in church, there was always a time for pastoral prayer included in the Sunday and Wednesday evening worship services, but this is rare these days.

Pastoral counseling — Biblical counseling is the best form of counseling you as a pastor can provide individuals, since you will normally not be a trained mental health counselor. There will be times when you will need to refer a person to a competent Christian counselor.

Benevolence ministry — You will have opportunities to provide benevolent care when you learn that people need assistance with food, clothing, shelter, medical bills, and the like. Beyond the church, there are Christian organizations involved in benevolence ministries.

Crisis intervention — People will often turn to pastors in times of personal and community crisis. Like a chaplain, you will need to be prepared to minister to people going through extreme crises.

Pastoral visitation — No area of pastoral ministry is more neglected today than pastoral visiting. One of the most prominent preachers in Baptist history, R.G. Lee, known for his sermon "Payday Someday," found time every day in was in the city, to make brief pastoral calls. Opportunities for church visits include the following:

— Church member home visits

— Visits at businesses, employment, social events

— Hospitals and rehab centers

— Nursing homes

— Death hour visits

— Church prospect visits in homes of non-members, especially those who visit your church and live in proximity of the church.

CHAPTER 9

COUNSELING LIKE JESUS

Jesus was a wise counselor to people needing spiritual guidance and counsel. He usually did His counseling in private sessions with individuals or groups. He has been called "the perfect psychologist" by a Christian psychologist and pastor.[1] It was prophesied that the Messiah would be called "a wonderful counselor" (Isa. 9:6), and indeed Jesus was a wonderful counselor. He counseled individuals in different ways depending upon the situation of the person or persons. At times, He confronted individuals with words of truth to set people free that were sometimes sharp and penetrating. Remember how He told Peter, "Get behind Me, Satan! You are an offense to Me, for you are not mindful of the things of God, but the things of men" (Matt. 16:23). Other times, He consoled the grief-stricken widow of Nain over her son who had died. Jesus had compassion on her and said to her, "Do not weep," then raised her son from death (Luke 7:11-15).

The Apostle Paul wrote the church in Rome, "We then who are strong have an obligation to bear the weaknesses of those without strength" (Rom. 15:1, HCSB). To the Galatians, Paul wrote, "Brethren, if a man is overtaken in any trespass, you who are spiritual restore such a

---

1 Bill Gaultiere, "Jesus' Ministry as the Wonderful Counselor," accessed February 2, 2022, https://www.soulshepherding.org/jesus-ministry-as-the-wonderful-counselor.

one in a spirit of gentleness considering yourself lest you also be tempted. Bear one another's burdens, and so fulfill the law of Christ" (Gal. 6:1-2). The law of Christ is love for neighbors by which we serve one another (Gal. 5:13-14). That love is manifested in the pastor's Christ-centered counseling ministries.

Down through the history of the church, counseling has been advocated spiritually in a number of ways in the New Testament with such commands to believers to "admonish one another" (Rom. 15:14); "encourage one another" (1 Thess. 5:11; Heb. 3:13); "comfort one another" (1 Thess. 4:18); "build up one another" (1 Thess. 5:11); confess your sins to one another and pray for one another" (James 5:16). Christ-followers have a responsibility to encourage and guide other believers when they are troubled. A verse that has always spoken to me when counseling and visiting with troubled people is James 1:5: "If any of you lacks wisdom, let him ask of God, who gives to all liberally and without reproach, and it will be given him."

Christians from time to time develop unresolved personal issues in their lives, and they want to talk with someone they hope will listen understandingly and help them solve their problems. A pastor will often be turned to for counsel, since he shepherds God's flock and is assumed to have some training in counseling. God's spiritual leaders provided pastoral care and counseling throughout the Bible. God Himself is portrayed as a gentle shepherd who cares for and comforts His flock with tenderness and love (Isa. 40:11). A pastor cannot tend Jesus' sheep and neglect counseling duties, even though many pastors do not like counseling ministry.

People will consult the pastor about such concerns as singleness, marriage and family crises, children, finances, health, grief, anxiety, worry, depression, discouragement, moral failures, guilt, assurance of salvation, decision making, human relations conflicts with people, and anything they feel troubled about. Pastors as God's servants ministering the Word of God need wisdom when helping people deal with the troubling issues in their lives.

Speaking of the key ingredient of wisdom needed in counseling, Proverbs 8:14 says, "Counsel is mine, and sound wisdom; I am understanding, I have strength." There is nothing pastors need more in their shepherding role than the love and wisdom of Jesus in counseling people with the commitment to "speak the truth in love" (Eph. 4:15).

Pastoral Counseling Is Biblically Based

Pastoral counseling for a pastor takes place in the context of a ministry based upon the Scriptures. Since the 1960s, Christian psychological counseling has become very popular with pastors and ministry associates who often use techniques and therapies from the behavioral sciences, blending Scripture with secular sources. This trend "has opened the door to a whole range of extra-biblical theories and therapies. Indeed, it has left many with the feeling that God's Word is incomplete, insufficient, unsophisticated, and unable to offer help for people's deepest emotional and spiritual problems."[2]

Biblical counseling is a Godward focus toward solving people's problems. It is about discovering the causes of their problems and then applying biblical principles to those causes. Biblical counseling rests upon the Sufficiency of Scripture (God's Word is truth that can be trusted) and the Superiority of Scripture (God's Word is superior to anything the world has to offer in terms of advice and problem solving for human issues). Hebrews 4:12: "For the word of God is living and

---

2 John MacArthur, Wayne Mack, and the Master's College Faculty, *Introduction to Biblical Counseling* (Nashville: Thomas Nelson, 1994), 4. An updated book by John MacArthur and the Master's College Faculty is *Counseling: How to Counsel Biblically* (Nashville: Thomas Nelson, 2005).

powerful, and sharper than any two-edged sword, piercing even to the division of soul and spirit, and of joints and marrow, and is a discerner of the thoughts and intents of the heart."

Biblical counseling is based upon the premise of the Inspiration, Authority, and Sufficiency of Scripture. God's Word is truth without any mixture of error, and people are made free by truth (John 17:17, 8:31-32). Pastors are called and commissioned to be Christ's instruments of changing lives with His unchanging truth, the Word of God. The Apostle Paul wrote Timothy, "All Scripture is given by inspiration of God, and is profitable for doctrine, for reproof, for correction, for instruction in righteousness, that the man of God may be complete, thoroughly equipped for every good work" (2 Tim. 2:15-16).

Some Principles of Biblical Pastoral Counseling

The following thoughts about biblical counseling are in no way a complete course on the subject. Some seminaries offer a course on biblical counseling, and, from time to time, short-course certificate training on the subject.

The bottom line is this: A biblical pastoral counselor counsels in the context of the teachings of the Bible and the resources of the spiritual life centered in Jesus Christ. This means you will:

Listen patiently, carefully, and empathetically to what the person shares with you. Pastors are typically good at speaking but not so good at listening. You must discipline yourself to listen intently and ask open-ended questions to try to get to the root of the person's issue or problem. James said to "be quick to listen, slow to speak" (James 1:19, NIV).

Consider what the person shares in relation to the teachings of Scripture and the way of Christ. The gospel of Jesus Christ is the first step to helping people solve the problems they bring to you. In the counseling session, listen and think narratively. While hearing their story, ask the Holy Spirit to bring to mind what story, what person, what situation, or even what principles in the Bible does this person's situation most connect with.

When those things have been brought to your mind by the Holy Spirit, share the story or the passage with them. Once you've shared the story or that passage, ask two questions: (1) Does that story relate to your situation? (2) Tell me how it does, or tell me why it does not.

Encourage the person to reflect upon God's Word about their situation and to make changes that are necessary in their life. The counselee may need to be advised to read, study, memorize, and meditate upon Scripture in relation to the issues(s) he or she is dealing with. Second Timothy 2:15: "Study [be diligent] to present yourself approved to God, a worker who does not need to be ashamed, rightly dividing [cutting straight] the word of truth."

Develop a compassionate approach with the counselee. The following are some suggestions on how to do this, discussed in more detail in John MacArthur's *Introduction to Biblical Counseling*:[3]

- Think about how you would feel if you were in the counselee's position. Jesus was "moved with compassion" (Matt. 9:36; Luke 7:13).
- Think of the counselee as a family member. In reality, our counselees are our spiritual brothers and sisters in Christ, and our Heavenly Father demands they be treated as such (1 Tim. 5:1-2).
- Think about your own sinfulness and know that you, too, have been tempted and have sinned (Gal. 6:1).
- Think about practical ways to show compassion (Luke 6:27-28).

---

3 MacArthur, *Introduction to Biblical Counseling*, 175-79.

Show respect to the counselees in the way you communicate with them.
- Use proper verbal communication (Eph. 4:15).
- Use proper nonverbal communication (Lev. 19:32).
- Take the counselee's problems seriously. Never minimize the problems presented by your counselees.
- Trust your counselees (1 Cor. 13:7).
- Express confidence in the counselee (2 Cor. 7:16).
- Welcome the counselee's input.
- Maintain confidentiality. Guard their reputations as much as possible without disobeying God; however, this is not always possible if the church needs to be told a believer will not repent after private and small group confrontation (Matt. 18:16-17).

Offer realistic biblical hope to counselees. Believers who come to you with problems need hope, a hope based upon spiritual truth and realities. False hope is typically based on human ideas of what is pleasurable and desirable, a denial of reality, mystical or magical thinking, or an improper interpretation of Scripture, and an unbiblical view of prayer.

True hope is a biblically based expectation of good based on the promises of God; true hope is the result of true salvation; is realistic, must be renewed daily, and is inseparable from a diligent and accurate study of God's Word.[4]

Teach the counselee to think biblically. Think biblically about the specific situation, God's character, the possibilities for good, the divine resources, the nature and cause of the problem, and what they say. MacArthur's book gives more good advice about biblical counseling.[5]

---

4 MacArthur, *Introduction to Biblical Counseling*, 189-99.
5 Ibid., 202-07.

When necessary, confront sin and admonish the counselee to confess and repent of any attitudes and actions contrary to Christ. It is the Holy Spirit's role to guide believers into all truth (John 16:13) and to convict the believer of sin, righteousness, and judgment (John 16:8). If the Holy Spirit does not indwell a person's life, biblical counseling will not help resolve the problems that brought the individual for help.

Only the Holy Spirit working in relation to God's Word can bring about fundamental changes in the human heart. First John 1:9: "If we confess our sins, He is faithful and just to forgive us our sins and to cleanse us from all unrighteousness." James 5:16: "Confess your trespasses to one another, and pray for one another, that you may be healed. The effective, fervent prayer of a righteous man avails much." As a pastor, you must be a trusted person with whom the individual can share their sin issues. Above all, keep confidences. Most of what is shared with you will have to be taken to the grave.

Pray for the individuals you counsel with. Always end the session with prayer; you may even want to pray about something during the time of counseling. Even if the conversation feels that it resolved nothing, pray. Pray for the person, commit to pray for him or her. It has been said that it is greater to speak to the Father about men than to speak to men about the Father.Pastoral counseling can easily become complex. The kingdom is greatly served when we keep boundaries, know our limits, and move people to the Word and prayer.

Refer the counselee to other trained counselors when their issue(s) are beyond your training and ability to help the person. Do not hesitate to refer individuals with serious physical problems to medical doctors, mental issues to competent Christian mental health counselors, or abuse situations to proper authorities. All states have laws against child abuse, and by law you must report those cases. Remember, you are a pastor and not a physician, lawyer, social worker, or professional mental health counselor. Know your limits and stay in your lane.

General Policies About Pastoral Counseling

Pastoral counseling should always be done with an open door or with a large window in the door. I served on the church staff of a large church once, and the pastor's office at the end of the long rectangular office building was completely glass so that anyone could see the pastor and the counselee but not hear the conversation. His secretary's desk was immediately beside his office in view of him and the counselee at all times. In the military as a chaplain, we had to have a glass window in the door or a chaplain's assistant nearby with the door opened.

There are pastoral counseling teachers who advise students and pastors not to counsel women but to counsel either couples or just the husband. James Bryant writes, "The best advice ever given to me by older pastors was never to counsel a woman alone without either your wife or another person present."[6] The reasons are: (1) appearances in relation to the possibility of accusations and (2) the woman's marital status such that a pastor's counsel may come between her and her husband's counsel.

Pastors should not do ongoing counseling. John Bisagno has a strong view about pastors involved in ongoing counseling. He writes, "The person whose needs cannot be met in one session should be referred to a professional. God-called and well-trained family counselors abound. Take every opportunity to refer … Pastors who spend hours a week in counseling should go into the full-time counseling ministry. Twenty hours a week invested in counseling will leave little time for your personal spiritual development, study, and family, let alone any

---

6 James W. Bryant and Mac Brunson, *The New Guidebook for Pastors* (Nashville: B&H, 2007), 159.

time to meet the expanding needs of a growing church and a lost world."[7]

Some pastoral counseling professors have recommended micro counseling or brief counseling. Wayne Oates, in *Protestant Pastoral Counseling*, makes recommendations regarding three functions of "brief visits." James Bryant summarizes, "First, a brief visit may help a counselee turn the corner. Talking helps. It helps a person to clarify things and map out a path to help solve problems. Second, brief visits are supportive counseling. It is good to know that someone is standing by to help. Third, brief visits can do no harm. In fact, a brief visit may be more advantageous than prolonged counseling, especially in a small town … in a small community, extended counseling is likely to be misunderstood."[8]

Don't let people pour out the details of their sin to you. Dr. W.A. Criswell, when I went to his School of the Prophets at First Baptist Church of Dallas in 1974, made this point in a session, quoted in what James Bryant wrote: "Don't let people pour out the sordid details of their sin to you. It may help them, but it will defile your mind, and eventually you will lose those people."[9] It is not a good idea for pastors to counsel with church members regarding details of infidelity because afterward when the individuals are sitting in the congregation, they will be reminded they discussed these things with their pastor, and it might cause them to leave the church. I personally think the counseling of sexual immorality of church members should be referred to a professional biblical counselor.

Literature on Biblical Counseling

Here are some good resources for you to refer to regarding biblical and Christian counseling:

---

7 John Bisagno, *Pastor's Handbook* (Nashville: B&H, 2011), 129.
8 Bryant and Brunson, *The New Guidebook for Pastors*, 158.
9 Ibid., 157.

- Babler, John, and Nicolas Ellen. *Counseling by the Book, Revised and Expanded*. Fort Worth: CTW, 2019.
- Clinton, Tim and Ron Hawkins. *The Quick-Reference Guide to Biblical Counseling*. Grand Rapids: Zondervan, 2009.
- Lambert, Heath. *A Theology of Biblical Counseling: The Doctrinal Foundations of Counseling Ministry*. Grand Rapids: Zondervan, 2016.
- Lelek, Jeremy. *Biblical Counseling Basics: Roots, Beliefs, Future*. Greensboro, NC: New Growth Press, 2018.
- MacArthur, John F. Jr., Wayne A. Mack, and the Master's College Faculty. *Introduction to Biblical Counseling: A Basic Guide to the Principles and Practice of Counseling*. Nashville: W. Publishing Group, 1994.
- MacArthur, John and the Master's College Faculty. *Counseling: How to Counsel Biblically*. Nashville: Thomas Nelson, 2005.
- MacDonald, James, Bob Kellemen and Steve Viars. *Christ-Centered Biblical Counseling: Changing Lives With God's Changeless Truth*. Eugene, OR: Harvest House, 2013.
- Paulison, David. *The Biblical Counseling Movement: History and Context*. Greensboro, NC: New Growth Press, 2010.

Literature on Christian Counseling

Through the years, I have referred to these sources in the attempt to better understand people and the issues they brought to me as a pastor, chaplain, and professor:

- Clinton, Tim and Ron Hawkins. *The Popular Encyclopedia of Christian Counseling*. Eugene, OR: Harvest House, 2011.
- Collins, Gary. *Christian Counseling: A Comprehensive Guide*, 3rd Edition. Nashville: Nelson Reference & Electronics, 2007.

- Narramore, Clyde M. *Encyclopedia of Psychological Problems.* Grand Rapids: Zondervan, 1966.
- _____. *The Psychology of Counseling.* Grand Rapids: Zondervan, 1960.

CHAPTER 10

CONDUCTING CHURCH MINISTRY BUSINESS

Reading through the four Gospels, we learn very little about Jesus conducting meetings with the disciples and others who followed Him, but there were surely times when He met with them to plan and discuss ministry strategy before sending out the Twelve and the Seventy (Matt. 10:5-15; Mark 6:7-13; Luke 10:1-16). As a pastor, you will spend many hours in congregational, committee, and church staff meetings. We see this clearly in two passages in the Acts of the Apostles. In Acts 6:1-6, a Jerusalem church meeting was called to deal with a complaint from the Hellenistic Jews against the Hebraic Jews because the Hellenistic widows were being overlooked in the daily distribution of food. The apostles gathered the church and asked the disciples to choose from among them seven men known to be full of the Spirit and wisdom to assume the responsibility for this ministry. The proposal pleased the whole church, and the seven men were presented to the apostles to pray for them and lay hands on them.

In Acts 15:1-29, we read about another important church meeting in Jerusalem called to discuss the issue of circumcision in relation to salvation for Gentiles. Some individuals from Judea came to the Antioch church in Syria and began teaching doctrine contrary to what Paul and Barnabas had been teaching. Paul, Barnabas, and some other believers were appointed to go to Jerusalem to see the apostles and elders about this matter. En route from Antioch, the men traveled through Phoenicia and Samaria and shared how Gentiles had been converted to Christ. Upon arrival in Jerusalem, they were welcomed by the congregation, and they shared with the apostles and elders what God had been doing through them.

Then the apostles and elders called a meeting to discuss the theological issue of whether the position of the Pharisees that Gentiles must be circumcised and required to obey the law of Moses was to be approved. In the meeting, the Apostle Peter stood and gave a testimony of how God revealed that He accepted the Gentiles by giving them the Holy Spirit, just as had been given to Jews who put their faith in Christ. Peter said, "We believe it is through the grace of our Lord Jesus that we are saved, just as they are" (Acts 15:11).

The whole congregation became silent as Barnabas and Paul shared about the miraculous signs and wonders God had done among the Gentiles through them. Then James, senior leader of the Jerusalem church, stood and quoted the Old Testament passage from Amos 9:11-12 that led him to advise that the church should not make it difficult for Gentiles turning to God, but that they should be instructed to abstain from food polluted by idols, from sexual immorality, from the meat of strangled animals, and from blood.

James's advice was accepted, and the apostles and elders — with the consent of the church — sent Judas (called Barsabbas) and Silas with Paul and Barnabas to deliver to the Gentile believers at Antioch a letter saying that unauthorized individuals had gone out from the Jerusalem church with an unapproved message, and the Gentile believers were not required to be circumcised; however, they were to practice certain stipulated moral and religious spiritual disciplines mentioned above.

Like the apostles and James, you will need to know the Scriptures and how they may be applied by the Holy Spirit to the contrary issues that come up in the church. The challenges of ministry will cause you to compare spiritual things with spiritual things (1 Cor. 2:13), Scripture with Scripture, under the leadership of the Holy Spirit.

Conducting Church Business

The New Testament does not reveal much specific guidance on how the early church conducted business. The Acts of the Apostles gives us some basic principles employed by the earliest church in Jerusalem.

Acts 1:15-26. Concerns the selection of an apostle to take the place of Judas Iscariot. From approximately 120 disciples, two men — Justus and Matthias — were determined to be qualified, having followed Jesus from the baptism of John until Jesus died, rose again, and ascended to heaven. These two were witnesses of the resurrection of Jesus. After prayer, lots were cast, and Matthias became the replacement apostle for Judas. Whether the casting of lots was like a vote for or against one or the other, or something equivalent to a coin flip, we do not know — but the Lord guided the process after prayer.

Acts 6:1-6. Tells of the election of seven men to assist the apostles. When an issue arose in the Jerusalem church about the daily distribution of the food to the widows, the apostles called together the multitude of disciples and asked them to seek from the congregation seven men of good reputation, full of the Holy Spirit and wisdom, whom the apostles could appoint over this business. Seven men were selected by the multitude and set before the apostles. After prayer, the apostles laid lands on the seven men, who began to handle this ministry so that the apostles could give themselves to prayer and the ministry of the Word. Here we see a congregational form of decision-making in the Jerusalem church.

Acts 13:1-3. Relates that while several church leaders were ministering to the Lord and fasting, the Holy Spirit instructed them to set apart Barnabas and Saul (Paul) for the work God had called them to do. After more fasting and prayer, hands were laid on Barnabas and Paul, and the church sent them on their mission — and they went to Cyprus, Antioch in Pisidia, Iconium, Lystra, and Derbe.

Acts 14:27. Tells that when Paul and Barnabas returned from the First Missionary Journey, the church gathered and heard their missionary report, what God had done through them, and how churches were planted.

Acts 15:22. Relates the mission to deliver the decision of the Jerusalem Council about evangelism of the Gentiles, a decision by the apostles, elders, and the whole church gathered to send Paul, Barnabas, Judas (Barsabbas), and Silas to the Antioch church with the decree of the Jerusalem Council.

Congregational Church Government

Even though God used Spirit-filled leaders in the work of the church, the earliest form of church government appears to be congregational government. This form of governing the church reflects the body life referred to in Romans 12:5: "So we, being many, are one body in Christ, and individually members of one another."

Congregationalism speaks of a form of church government. "Episcopal" church government is rule by bishops. "Presbyterian" church government is rule by the elders. "Congregational" church government is rule by the congregation under Christ administered by the leaders of the church. This does not mean that members of the church must have the permission of the church to share Christ and do ministry in His name.

Episcopal government usually includes a hierarchy over the local church. Presbyterian government sometimes does as well via elders. Congregational government nearly always avoids such hierarchy, maintaining that the local church is answerable directly to God, not to some man or organization. Congregational government is found in many Baptist and independent non-denominational churches. Churches with congregational government will normally be led by pastors, elders, and deacons called out and commissioned by the local church.

The key issue for church government is the lordship of Christ. Jesus Christ is Lord of His church, and the Holy Spirit will guide in the decisions made by the Body of Christ. If members of the church are filled with the Spirit, the Holy Spirit will guide them to honor Christ and God's Word in decisions affecting the whole church. Congregational church government is based upon the following scriptural principles:

The lordship of Christ (Eph. 4:15; Phil. 2:11) — Christ is the true head of the church.

The authority of the Bible (2 Tim. 3:16-17) — God's Word should guide the decisions of the church.

Salvation by grace through faith (Eph. 2:8-10) — The ground is level at the foot of the cross; therefore, no Christian is to lord over another. The church is to be ultimately governed under the lordship of Christ. The Word of God and the Holy Spirit provide guidance for the church.

Soul competency and the priesthood of believers (1 Pet. 2:9; Rev. 5:1-10) — Each believer-priest has direct access to God through the Scriptures and prayer, and is free under the guidance of the Holy Spirit to determine God's will; each believer is a part of a royal priesthood, of which Jesus Christ is the High Priest (Heb. 7-10).

Regenerate church membership of baptized believers — Church government should not be in the hands of one or a few, but in the body of born-again baptized believers. The Holy Spirit lives in every true believer in the church (1 Cor. 12:13).

Polity of the Church

An examination of the New Testament evidence reveals two very clear elements in the polity (form of government) of the church: (1) The churches of the New Testament period were independent, self-governing assemblies of believers that appointed their own leaders, determined their own customs, and settled their own difficulties; (2) churches were democratically ruled, in which members had a voice in the major decisions of the church.

Early New Testament churches often differed in organization, form of worship and leadership. The spiritual leaders (bishops, elders, pastors) assisted by deacons led out and conducted the ministry of the church theologically, spiritually, and morally, trusting the gathered church to make good decisions affecting the entire membership. Of course, it is not practical for the total membership of the church to be involved in every decision of ministry; therefore, churches follow a variety of policies and procedures in carrying out the business of the church.

In America today, many churches formalize administrative procedures in a **Constitution and Bylaws**. Ideally, all members are encouraged to participate in **Church Business Meetings.** In many churches, regular business meetings are held following a worship service or on Wednesday night and take place periodically, often quarterly. Special called business meetings are held for major non-routine matters such as voting on a committee recommendation for a new pastor, staff member, to adopt the annual budget or make changes to it, and to begin building projects.

Constitutions and Bylaws

A **Constitution and Bylaws** helps a church to carry out the biblical inunctions found in 1 Corinthians 14:33, 41: "For God is not the author of confusion but of peace, as in all the churches of the saints … Let all things be done decently and in order." A Constitution and Bylaws provides written guidelines to assist a church in moving toward the attainment of its God-called purpose. Sample church constitutions and bylaws may be viewed online.

A **church constitution** usually contains a preamble, a basic statement of purpose or objective, the legal name of the church, a statement of doctrinal beliefs, a church covenant, and a statement of basic denominational relationships or affiliations. The **bylaws** usually state how a church is organized to conduct its work, qualifications for membership and dismissal, congregational procedures for conducting church business, and duties of the church program leaders. Such documents are not necessary for a church to function, but churches have found that a constitution and bylaws can be helpful in conducting their work effectively.

Churches may or may not be **incorporated.** However, in today's complex and litigious climate in America, a church will usually benefit legally from incorporation. Do remember that laws and requirements differ from state to state, so it is best to consult with a reputable attorney and/or an associational director who coordinates denominational ministry for advice regarding incorporation and approval as a 501(c)(3) IRS non-profit organization.

Congregational Meetings

Baptist and independent churches typically conduct regular church business meetings once a month, once a quarter, or whenever the bylaws call for regular meetings. Provisions are usually included for how "special meetings" may be called to transact business in the interim period.

In some churches, the bylaws stipulate that the pastor preside over the meetings. In other churches, "an elected moderator" serves. In the churches I served as pastor, I always conducted the meetings myself since it was either required by the bylaws or expected according to the tradition of the church. While I served as a military chaplain and became a member of a large congregation (First Baptist Church of Columbia, South Carolina), a highly competent Christian layman (an attorney) moderated the meetings very adequately.

A typical business meeting of the congregation may be conducted in the following manner:

Quorum and Call to Order. The first step is to determine if there is a quorum present — the requirement for a quorum is usually stated in the bylaws; if so, declare a quorum present and call the meeting to order, followed by a Scripture reading and prayer. During the time for Scripture reading and prayer, the pastor has the opportunity to remind the congregation that the meeting is for the purpose of conducting God's business according to the principles of the Word of God and the leadership of the Holy Spirit. Let the people know that God is present, and that He will guide the meeting if we allow Him. Pray that God will be glorified in the way in which the meeting is conducted. The lordship of Christ must guide the meeting.

Minutes. Next, call for the reading or distribution of the minutes from the previous meeting and any meeting(s) since the last regular business meeting. Declare the minutes approved as read (or printed) and corrected if there are corrections. A vote is not necessary.

Reports. Then, call for reports: Treasurer, Sunday School, Discipleship Training, Deacons, Church Council, Music Committee, Building and Grounds Committee, Budget and Finance Committee, or any other committee. The church does not need to vote to approve these reports unless a report calls for action or sets forth recommendations to be considered by the church. I think it is best to handle all old and new business from the committees at the stated time for such. Reports furnish information on accomplishments by the committees.

Old (Unfinished) Business. The minutes or the church clerk will normally remind the moderator of any unfinished business that may need action.

New Business. I favor all new business be sent to the moderator in advance of the meeting to be put on a written agenda. Start with motions from the deacons, the church council, and committees. Action always requires a motion, a second (unless it comes from a committee), discussion, and vote. Most routine business votes require only a majority vote. Smaller Baptist churches usually allow church members to initiate business from the floor, and very often the member will just want to introduce or discuss an issue or talk about an opportunity for ministry without placing it in the form of a motion.

Miscellaneous Business. Reserve some time for miscellaneous business that may be put on the agenda or may be initiated by an individual member from the floor. Miscellaneous Business can be risky. In the smaller churches I served as pastor, during Miscellaneous Business I would say, "This is your opportunity to be a committee of one and introduce business that may need to be considered by the church body." You would ask the person to put the item of miscellaneous business into the form of a motion. Then call for a second to the motion. Individuals will speak in turn for and against the motion before a vote. Large churches are generally not going to do this.

One possibility if the motion of new business or miscellaneous business needs to be discussed much more formally or at greater length than in a regular meeting, the motion may be referred to a committee or perhaps to the executive board of your church by adopting a subsidiary motion to commit. In other words, it is possible to refer this motion to an appropriate committee for study, prayer, and action at a later time. Sometimes you will sense that there is a consensus on an item of miscellaneous business, and it will need to be voted on at that time.

Announcements. After all business is conducted, you will want to share announcements and the date of the next regular business meeting.

Adjournment. Finally, ask for a motion to adjourn, followed by a second. Thereupon, I would usually say, "All in favor, please stand for closing prayer."

Closing Prayer. Either close the meeting yourself in prayer or call on someone.

Dismissal. Declare the meeting adjourned.

Motions in Congregational Meetings

Many churches have adopted the most current edition of *Robert's Rules of Order Newly Revised* by Henry M. Robert. However, our modern congregational meetings must not be so much about business as about the mission and ministry of the church — the Lord's business. The Rules of Order simply provide guidance for orderly meetings.

Barry McCarty, parliamentarian for the Southern Baptist Convention and currently a professor at Southwestern Baptist Theological Seminary, has written an excellent guide for churches, entitled *A Parliamentary Guide for Church Leaders* (2012). This is the best material in print for Baptist and independent church pastors. On pages 19-24, McCarty suggests six general principles for deliberative assemblies:

1. Group decision should be made in an orderly fashion.
2. The majority rules.
3. The minority must not be suppressed.
4. Every member has the right to be heard and to hear what other members have to say.
5. All members have equal rights, privileges, and responsibilities.
6. Members have a right to know what is going on.

Four principles of parliamentary law in congregational meetings

should exist for Christian harmony to prevail:
1. Christian courtesy and justice for all — fairness.
2. Consider one thing at a time. I made a big mistake once at a Baptist state convention by introducing two motions at the same time. The moderator corrected me about this.
3. The minority must be heard.
4. The majority must prevail.

The moderator must be neutral and insist that Christians who have different opinions on issues agree to disagree agreeably — that all things be done decently and in order (1 Cor. 14:40). The moderator will set the tone! Remember John 17 — on spiritual unity. Show respect for all opinions and all sides of an issue. Remind the church to seek the mind of Christ (1 Cor. 2:16) on all matters. The church is not a pure democracy but a Christocracy — government under Christ: He is the true head of the church (Eph. 5:23). In all things, Christ must have the preeminence (Col. 1:18).

The presiding officer (moderator) must never enter the debate or discussion while occupying the chair. A presiding moderator must not take sides in a discussion. If he must speak to a motion, he must yield the chair, but this should be rare. A moderator must not work the system to get his own way. His job is not to manage the outcome of the meeting but to conduct the meeting fairly under Christ. The pastor-moderator is not always right about all things and every decision the church will make.

The pastor, remember, is the pastor of all the people and must shepherd all the people. Deep feelings can emerge during business meetings over controversial issues. This is the reason it is best for the pastor not to moderate if there is a qualified and experienced (mature, balanced, fair) member to moderate the meetings. However, in small church situations, the pastor is often the most qualified and will have to preside. Attending associational meetings, state conventions, and the Southern Baptist Convention or other Baptist national convention meetings provide good opportunities to learn how to successfully conduct church business meetings. You can learn much by observation and participation.

A person making reports normally should stand and face the congregation; however, in small churches this may not always happen. Motion makers stand and face the moderator. Likewise, those discussing the issues should face the moderator; they are not making speeches to the congregation or their supporters. During the time for discussion, always make sure that accurate facts are presented — strive to discover *what* is right and not *who* is right. Keep personalities out of the issue. People sometimes do not have accurate statistics to support their point, so you may want to inquire about the source of the statistics.

Work hard not to have close votes. Rather than forcing close votes and polarizing/dividing the church, I recommend calling for a motion to table the motion and send the issue to an appropriate committee for more study and prayer. If there is not an appropriate committee, you could create an ad-hoc committee to deal with the specific issue.

Technically, tabling is not correct according to Robert's Rules, but this is often what churches do by tradition. The motion is really a motion to postpone action. If discussion (for and against) seems to suggest that there is a serious division among church members on an issue, it is best to entertain a motion to postpone the motion to a specific time, reconsider, or send the motion to a committee for further study and prayer. This would be a subsidiary motion.

Motions to hold down debate (end, limit or extend) require a two-thirds vote. Likewise, a motion to close nominations requires a two-thirds vote. This would happen, for example, when someone says, "I move nominations cease" or "I move that nominations cease, and

Brother Smith be elected by acclamation" if only one nomination is offered. A member may withdraw the motion "before it is stated" by the chairman before the vote. The moderator must say, "The maker of the motion wishes to withdraw the motion. If there are no objections, he (or she) will be permitted to withdraw the motion. Are there any objections? Hearing none, the chair declares it withdrawn."

The presiding officer must state the motion clearly before putting the motion to a vote, and he must state clearly the results of the vote. After discussion, the moderator should not ask, "Are you ready to vote?" or "Are you ready for the question?" Instead, the moderator should say, "Hearing no further discussion, we are voting on the motion that [state the motion] … All in favor say Aye. All opposed say No." If the majority votes favorably, say, "The Ayes have it and the motion carries." If the majority votes No, say, "The motion fails." Moderators typically ask for people to raise hands or to stand. Sometimes individuals call for a secret ballot, and you will have to make arrangements for such with ballots and individuals to count the votes.

Subsidiary Motions

Here is a brief list of subsidiary motions that may be employed in business meetings:

To lay on the table — to lay aside a pending motion temporarily while other more urgent business is handled.

To call for the previous question — a motion to stop debate when there is needless repetition of argument; a second and a two-thirds vote required.

To limit (or extend) debate — to limit debate to less than ten minutes per speaker or to extend time for each speaker; a two-thirds vote required.

To postpone definitely (to a later specified time) — this requires a second, is debatable and requires a majority vote to carry.

To commit or refer to committee — to send to a smaller group or committee; could have the instruction to report back at the next meeting; this requires a second, is debatable, and is amendable.

To amend — a second is required, debatable, and a majority vote is required. An amendment can delete words, phrases, sentences or paragraphs, strike out words, phrases or sentences and insert new ones; add words, phrases, sentences, or paragraphs; or substitute an entire paragraph(s) or an entire text of the motion and insert another.

To postpone indefinitely — to kill a main motion without bringing the main motion to a vote. This requires a second, is debatable, is not amendable, and requires a majority vote to carry.

CHAPTER 11

WORSHIP, PREACHING, EVANGELISM, MISSIONS, CHURCH PLANTING

In John 4:1-26, we read of the time, about noon at Jacob's well, when Jesus had an encounter with a Samaritan woman in which He had an exchange with her about living water leading to the everlasting life that He offered. Then she turned the conversation to differences in the place of worship, since Samaritans worshiped on Mount Gerizim while the Jews worshiped at the temple in Jerusalem.

Jesus told her that the hour was coming when she would not worship on Mount Gerizim or in Jerusalem. He told her that she did not know the true nature of worship and that "the hour is coming, and now is, when the true worshipers will worship the Father in spirit and truth, for the Father is seeking such to worship Him. God is Spirit, and those who worship Him must worship in spirit and truth" (John 4:23-24).

More important than the place for worship is knowing the Lord and having the right condition of the heart. Heart condition is still an issue today for people who attend worship out of habit, going through the motions of worship while their heart and life are far from knowing God and His Son (Isa. 29:13; Ezek. 33:3; Matt. 15:8; Mark 7:6). Years ago, A.W. Tozer called worship "the missing jewel of the church."

Worship in churches from the first century to this day is a gathering of God's people to bow their hearts and lives before Him in honor, praise, adoration, obedience, and thanks for who He is, what He has done, what He is doing, and what He is going to do. We worship God through singing psalms, hymns, spiritual songs, praying, and listening to God's Word being proclaimed and explained.

Preaching and teaching the Word of God, evangelism, missions, and church planting were priorities in the early church. The Apostle Paul wrote his associate Timothy to "Preach the word! Be ready in season and out of season. Convince, rebuke, exhort, with all longsuffering and doctrine" (2 Tim. 4:2, KJV). People are saved through belief in the "foolishness of the message preached" (1 Cor. 1:21, KJV). For this reason, the Apostle Paul wrote Timothy in his first letter to him to "teach and preach these principles" (1 Tim. 6:2, NASB). And this will be done through evangelism, missions, and church planting.

Worship

One of the primary responsibilities of the pastor is to plan and lead worship for the local church. This will certainly include Sunday morning and evening services, midweek evening services, and special worship services like Maundy Thursday, Good Friday, ordination services, and worship during Bible and missionary conferences, and evangelistic-revival-stewardship meetings. Funeral and marriage services are often planned as worship. Pastors may also be asked to plan community worship services like a Thanksgiving Eve service or when there have been serious crises in the community. I remember leading a community prayer and worship service as an Army chaplain at Fort Dix after the 2001 bombing of the Twin Towers of the World Trade Center in New York City.

True biblical worship (John 4:23-24) is observed in **spirit** (our spirit yielding to the Holy Spirit) and in **truth** (the Word of God guiding). In true worship, God's people bow their hearts and lives before the Lord in praise, adoration, and obedience (Rom. 12:1-2; Rev. 4:10-11). Genuine godly worship will transform worshipers as their minds are renewed and their lives are no longer conformed to this world (Rom. 12:1-2). True worship takes believers into the presence of the Lord such that when God is enthroned in our worship, His manifest presence and power are manifested.

The Bible contains no less than 600 references to worship. The purpose of worship is to focus on the God who has revealed Himself in many ways, but especially through the Scriptures (2 Tim. 3:15-17) and Jesus Christ (Heb. 1:1-2). Only God is worthy of our worship (Rev. 4:11, 5:12). We don't worship God for what we get out of it, but because He is worthy of worship. Would you want your child to love you only for what he or she could get out of you?

Warren Wiersbe offers a good definition of worship: "Worship is the believers' response of all that they are — mind, emotions, will, and body — to what God is and says and does. This response has its mystical side in subjective experience and its practical side in objective obedience to God's revealed will. Worship is a loving response that's balanced by the fear of the Lord, and it is a deepening response as the believer comes to know God better."[1] Jesus spoke to some scribes and Pharisees about their hypocrisy in worship when he quoted Isaiah, saying, "These people draw near to Me with their mouth, and honor Me with their lips, but their heart is far from Me. And in vain they worship Me … (Matt. 15:8-9; Mark 7:6-7). Vain worship is a danger in the church when people are habitually going through the rituals and rites of worship without a sense of worshiping God in spirit and in truth.

---

1 Warren W. Wiersbe, *Real Worship: Playground, Battle Ground, or Holy Ground?* (Grand Rapids: Baker, 2000), 26.

Worship by Christians through the centuries has featured praise through singing and testimonies, Scripture readings, prayers, offerings, and a preached message (Biblical exposition and instruction). Baptism and the Lord's Supper are observed from time to time as elements of worship. Many pastors follow the calendar of the church year, remembering Palm Sunday, Good Friday, Resurrection Sunday (Easter), Pentecost, and Advent (the four Sundays prior to Christmas).

Pastors in the United States often celebrate national events and build worship services from Scripture and American Christian church tradition around such special days as Mother's Day, Father's Day, Independence Day, Memorial Day, and Veterans Day, even though these are not biblical events.

Pastors must prayerfully plan and prepare worship services in coordination with music ministers, musicians, and others who will participate in the worship. Secretaries and administrative assistants will be involved in preparing church bulletins if the church still uses such. Media personnel will have to be consulted about what needs to be projected on the screens of the church (words to songs, Scripture verses and passages, and congregational announcements). Individuals responsible for baptisms and the Lord's Supper will need to be contacted and coordinated with.

Classic or Contemporary Worship

Churches in the last twenty or more years have experienced what has been called the "worship wars" between classic (traditional) and contemporary music, and other features of modern worship services to include non-traditional sermons, video clips, PowerPoints, creative lighting, standing for long periods of time during the music by the praise band, pulpit dress, removal of the organ and piano in favor of the keyboard, guitars, and drums. Pastors will have to work through these changes with congregational leaders, committees, and in business meetings. Many churches have either implemented classic and contemporary worship services or blended worship services.

Preaching

One of the most important assignments of a pastor is preaching the Word of God. Words cannot be said any better than what the Apostle Paul wrote to Timothy: "Preach the word! Be ready in season and out of season. Convince, rebuke, exhort, with all longsuffering and teaching, for the time will come when they will not endure sound doctrine, but according to their own desires, because they have itching ears, they will heap up for themselves teachers; and they will turn their ears away from the truth, and be turned aside to fables" (2 Tim. 4:2-4). John Bisagno said about preaching, "You can strike out almost anywhere else and survive. But fail here, and you'll lose the game."[2]

It is a great privilege and honor to feed the Body of Christ the Word of God that will build up the members of the congregation and win people to Christ. Good preaching must include teaching God's Word. Preaching is proclamation and exhortation; teaching is explanation and instruction. Preachers apply the word of God through reinforcing Scriptures, stories, illustrations, and strong emphasis on pertinent truths.

If you are going to be a preacher who gets people into the meat of the Word (the depth of Scripture), then you must "study (be diligent) to show (present) yourself approved to God, a worker who does not need to be ashamed, rightly dividing (cutting it straight) the word of truth" (2 Tim. 2:15).

The professor of preaching I had in seminary taught us students

---

2 John Bisagno, *Pastor's Handbook* (Nashville: B&H, 2011), 193.

to study one hour for every minute we would preach in the pulpit. I think thirty minutes would be more realistic in view of pastoral visitation, counseling, and the other administrative duties of a pastor. Jesus said, "Feed My sheep" (John 21:17), not "Inspire My sheep" or "Entertain My sheep." The Lord convicted me some years ago about using too much humor in the pulpit. I quit telling preacher jokes I read or heard from other preachers, concluding such frivolity takes away from the reality of the spiritual truth we are communicating.

Preachers and speakers today in some modern worship services promise health, wealth, contentment, and a problem-free life to all who will follow their teaching. Does this really honor the truth of the Word where persecution and suffering have been the experience of many Christians down through church history to this day?

The Apostle Peter wrote, "The word of the LORD endures forever. Now this is the word which by the gospel was preached to you" (1 Pet. 1:25). Proclaim and explain God's Word to the congregation with all your mind, heart, soul, and strength. When I was an Army chaplain at Fort Jackson, I used to listen to re-broadcasted sermons of Dr. Martin Luther King Jr. on Sunday evenings and often when King would begin to use advanced vocabulary and speak in deep concepts, I would hear a man's voice from the congregation say out loud, "Make it plain." One of my fellow chaplains grew up in Ebenezer Baptist Church in Atlanta where King served until his tragic death in 1968. One day I asked him who was it that would say "make it plain" while Dr. King was preaching. He laughed and said it was his father, Rev. Martin Luther King Sr., with whom King served as co-pastor. The point is well made — make your message plain so the people can understand it! I asked a deacon once in an Army chapel congregation at Fort Dix if my preached sermon was plain. He responded, "It was so plain that a fool could have understood it!" Bless him, I took that as a compliment.

Preparing the Sermon

There is no place for a lack of serious biblical study in pastoral ministry, remembering in the words of James and the writer of Hebrews how spiritual leaders will incur a stricter judgment: "My brethren, let not many of you become teachers, knowing that we shall receive a stricter judgment" (James 3:1); "… they [spiritual leaders] watch out for our souls, as those who must give account …" (Heb. 13:17).

A pastor must have a daily time with God for personal reading of the scriptures and prayer, with a separate time set apart for preparing messages. He will need a place for uninterrupted study with good resource books containing insights into the original biblical languages, commentaries, illustrations, and thematic Christian books. Dr. W.A. Criswell, when I went to his School of the Prophets in 1974, recommended that we do as he did and have the church secretary put in their schedule books that we as a pastor have an appointment with God from 6:00 a.m. until noon and we will be available for counseling and hospital visiting in the afternoon and house calls in the evening.

The internet nowadays has access to sermons and materials for sermons, but do not plagiarize from other preachers. If you quote another gospel minister, or anyone for that matter, give that person credit. Do your own study with the help of the Holy Spirit and develop messages that speak to the theological, spiritual, moral, and pastoral needs of the people of your congregation.

Sermons may be topical, textual, or expository. Some pastors like to preach through books in the Bible with a series of messages. As God leads you to a text, topic, or book to preach from, begin by prayerfully meditating upon the verses. Determine the central idea and condense it down to a single propositional statement. Many preachers develop preaching and teaching points from the proposition that may be spoken to by exposition, reinforcing scriptures, stories, illustrations, items from the daily news, and applications.

Move your message toward a decision from the hearers. Remember, communication is not what you necessarily say, but it is what the listener hears within his or her own mind and heart as you are speaking. Therefore, it is important for you to be clear and concise in what you say. Even explain words from Scripture that people may not be familiar with.

Preachers deliver their messages with a manuscript, notes, or extemporaneously. Dr. W.A. Criswell of First Baptist Church, Dallas, used to write out his sermons word for word. He would then review them in his office before he went to the pulpit, but he would leave the manuscript in his office, depending upon his memory and the creative work of the Spirit of God in his preaching. There are professors of preaching who teach students to only speak extemporaneously. However, Billy Graham and other effective preachers and pastors have preached very well with notes and manuscripts.

John Bisagno, a very effective preacher of the Word in his day, gives some good points below about delivering the message[3], with my thoughts added:

1. Don't overdo the outline. He recommends that principles make up the outline rather than overdoing alliteration. Avoid being cute and clever with alliteration.

2. Freshen your illustrations and use plenty of them. People pay attention to stories, so use up-to-date stories such as people may have read online or heard on a recent newscast. Billy Graham often quoted things he had read in the news. Jesus, remember, was a master storyteller of parables to make His spiritual points.

3. Don't use so many notes. Your own thoughts birthed by the Holy Spirit are easier to remember and share than what others have written.

---

3 Bisagno, *Pastor's Handbook*, 202-04.

Bisagno suggests you condense your sermon into a few key words and memorize them for the following reasons:

a. It increases your sense of authority and confidence.

b. It gives you better eye contact with people.

c. It (preaching without notes) allows more freedom and spontaneity.

d. It is more conducive to conversational preaching, which is in these days; oratory is out.

e. It will be easier to hold your message to thirty minutes, the attention span of most people.

f. It will allow you to be natural and be yourself; the best style for you is the person God made you when He created you in your mother's womb.[4]

Evangelism, Missions, Church Planting

Pastors have been gifted by the Lord with a variety of spiritual gifts (Rom. 12:3-8; 1 Cor. 12:1-11, 27-30; Eph. 4:7-16; 1 Pet. 4:10-11). Some gospel ministers have been very gifted in evangelism and missionary church planting like the Apostle Paul, Barnabas, and Silas. Pastors must certainly give attention to evangelism, missions, and church planting.

In Matthew 29:18-20, Jesus commissioned the disciples to evangelize and disciple people throughout the world, which they began to do as soon as they had received power from the Holy Spirit (Acts 2:1-4). Before Jesus ascended to heaven, He told the apostles, "But you shall receive power when the Holy Spirit has come upon you; and you shall be witnesses to Me in Jerusalem, and in all Judea and Samaria, and to the ends of the earth" (Acts 1:8). *Foxe's Book of Martyrs* tells the story of how the apostles went all over the known world to do evangelism, missions, and church planting, and all but John died doing it.

---

4 Bisagno, *Pastor's Handbook*, 202-04.

Evangelism and missions are tasks of the church and of every believer. Churches should not only be centers for worship but also have a priority for evangelism and missions, with a plan and program to win souls to Christ and establish new churches beyond the local church. Evangelism and missions may be promoted by the pastor when he is personally involved in evangelistic preaching, soul-winning visitation, and training Christians to share the gospel of Christ and the way of salvation with others, as well as challenging church members to be involved in mission activities.

Too many churches unfortunately have gotten away from a church visitation night or day like Saturday, when church and staff members go out in pairs to call on the visitors to the church and prospects who need the Lord and a good church. The pastor ought to be the first one out the door when organized visitation takes place. Some pastors I have known did their visiting on Saturdays. As a pastor, I would visit one or two nights a week and on Saturdays and Sunday afternoons.

In days past, churches conducted evangelistic and revival meetings often preached by visiting pastors and evangelists as opportunities for people to hear the gospel each day or night for a specified number of gatherings when they could repent, be converted, or be reclaimed for Christ. Before revival services I led in churches, I often read Charles Finney's *Revival Lectures* for inspiration and good ideas prior to the meetings. Some churches conduct annual mission conferences to hear missionaries share the work of Christ where they serve and have served around the world.

A church under Christ's leadership will be involved in calling out individuals willing to go as missionaries to foreign lands where the gospel of Christ has not been preached. It takes funds to train and send members of the church overseas, so a missionary program and funding should be part of the church budget to be promoted by the pastor.

It is good when churches organize a mission committee and a missionary budget for cooperative national and international mission projects beyond the local church. A global vision for sending out short-term and long-term missionaries is just as important for the church as a local vision, remembering how Jesus said, "Lift up your eyes and look at the fields, for they are already white for harvest!" (John 4:35). To the disciples, He said, "The harvest truly is plentiful, but the laborers are few. Therefore pray the Lord of the harvest to send out laborers into His harvest" (Matt. 9:37-38).

And nothing may be as life-changing for Christians as being involved on a mission trip. Many churches conduct mission trips for congregational volunteers each year. When a church sends people on mission trips and contributes regularly to missionary organizations, the gospel will go forth around the world. When a pastor preaches on the call to missions, God may well call individuals to volunteer to be trained and leave home for another place in the world to share the good news of Jesus Christ. Our own daughter and her husband were called to missionary service in a foreign country. They established a 501(c)(3) missions organization and raised their financial support. The missionary they serve with was led of the Lord after his retirement from business at age sixty-five to plant five churches in the Dominican Republic in the last eighteen years. At age eighty-two, he is still going strong with the mission he was called by God to launch and develop.

It is encouraging to learn about evangelistic pastors and churches planting associated or independent churches instead of attempting to grow the established church larger. Some visionary pastors and churches have also entered into relationships with declining churches in communities to revive them by providing ministry teams and resources.

CHAPTER 12

SPIRITUAL AND ADMINISTRATIVE LEADERSHIP

Spiritual leadership is a high calling from the Lord. The Apostle Paul wrote Timothy, "If any man desires to the office of overseer (or bishop), it is a fine work he desires to do" (1 Tim. 3:1 NASB). Jeremiah wrote, "Are you seeking great things for yourself? Do not seek them" (45:5 NASB). Jesus chose twelve spiritual leaders from all those who followed Him, eleven of which (plus one that replaced Judas) served Him faithfully until the end of their lives.

Most Christians do not rush into spiritual leadership — wondering if the man should seek the position or should the position seek the man, knowing how ambition has caused the downfall of leaders in the church through the centuries, beginning with Judas Iscariot. Church leaders have always known hardship, rejection, and persecution in doing the work of Christ on earth. But the rewards are great in the kingdom of God when spiritual leaders following Christ serve people. Paul wrote, "If anyone's work which he has built on it (the foundation of Jesus Christ) endures, he will receive a reward" (1 Cor. 3:14).

J. Oswald Sanders has written, "True greatness, true leadership, is found in giving yourself in service to others, not in coaxing or inducing others to serve you. True service is never without cost. Often it comes with a painful baptism of suffering."[1] To follow Jesus in spiritual leadership, having been sent out as sheep in the midst of wolves, pastors must be "wise as serpents, and harmless as doves" (Matt. 10:16).

Jesus taught a new standard of greatness in Mark 10:42-45: "You know that those who are considered rulers over the Gentiles lord it over them, and their great ones exercise authority over them. Yet it shall not be so among you; but whoever desires to become great among you shall be your servant. And whoever of you desires to be first shall be slave of all. For even the Son of man did not come to be served, but to serve, and to give His life a ransom for many."

Thinking about leadership, Samuel Brengle, the great Salvation Army revival preacher, once said, "One of the outstanding ironies of history is the utter disregard of ranks and titles in the final judgments men pass on each other. The final estimate of men shows that history cares not an iota for the rank or title a man has borne, or the office he has held, but only the quality of his deeds and the character of his mind and heart."[2]

Leading God's people as a pastor is indeed a privilege and honor, but it is a great challenge to do things right in the sight of the Lord. God has gifted men for the ability to shepherd His people (Eph. 4:11-12). John Bisagno says it so well: "Shepherds don't follow the flock; they lead the flock. But that leadership must be deserved, earned, and won by integrity, faithful ministry, true humility, godliness, and feeding the flock the Word of God. And that takes time. The longer you pastor a congregation in that spirit, the more freedom you will be granted to lead."[3] This chapter will consider pastoral leadership, church administration, and finances.

---

1 J. Oswald Sanders, *Spiritual Leadership: Principles of Excellence for Every Believer* (Chicago: Moody Press, 1967, 1980, 1994), 15.
2 C.W. Hall, *Samuel Logan Brengle* (New York: Salvation Army, 1933), 274.
3 John Bisagno, *Pastor's Handbook* (Nashville: B&H, 2011), 11.

Pastoral Leadership

Leadership is key and essential to the life, mission, and ministry of the church. Without it, the church flounders in direction and is not able to fulfill its Christ-centered purposes. God needs pastors who are spiritual leaders for His people. The Apostle Peter understood the calling to spiritual leadership when he wrote, "The elders who are among you I exhort, I who am a fellow elder and a witness of the sufferings of Christ, and also a partaker of the glory that will be revealed. Shepherd the flock of God which is among you, serving as overseers, not by compulsion but willingly, not for dishonest gain but eagerly; nor as being lords over those entrusted to you, but being examples to the flock; and when the Chief Shepherd appears, you will receive the crown of glory that does not fade away" (1 Pet. 5:1-4).

Shepherding is the pivotal analogy for pastoral ministry. Thomas Oden writes, "Christian ministry is energized by the pivotal conviction that Christ Himself ordained and established the pastoral office for the edification and guidance of the church."[4]

John Bisagno in "Being a Leader" shares five principles from Peter's exhortation to the church about spiritual leaders:[5]

1. Don't even think about being a leader unless you are certain God has called you. Be certain of God's call to lead and serve His flock, the church.

2. It is better to do a few things well, than many not too well at all. Peter only exhorted the elders to do two things: feed the flock (preach and teach the Word of God) and take oversight (give general direction to the work of the church).

3. *What* you do may not be as important as *how* you do it. Peter

---

4 Thomas Oden, *Pastoral Theology: Essentials of Ministry* (San Francisco: HarperSanFrancisco, 1983), 50.
5 Bisagno, *Pastor's Handbook,* 147-148.

shares in verses 2-3 how elders are to do their work: with humility, integrity, godliness, motivation, character, and attitude. Style is never a substitute for substance. Giftedness is never a substitute for godly character. Sadly, I have known of gifted preachers who became pastors and had to be removed from their positions because of unfaithfulness in conduct and doctrine.

4. Leadership holds sacred the trust of another. Verse 3 tells us it is God's flock that pastors lead. The church belongs to Christ, not to the pastor, elders, or deacons. We have nothing in the way of leadership and influence that is not given to us by God and granted by His people.

5. The rewards of leadership are later and greater than the price you pay. Verse 4 reminds us that someday the Chief Shepherd will reward those who have served Him faithfully with an unfading crown of glory. A special crown is promised to the faithful under-shepherd. Bisagno closes, "Your greatest joy will not be receiving that crown but seeing His joy as you lay it at His feet." He had that privilege when he died in August 2018.

When I taught pastoral theology, leadership, and ministry at Southwestern Baptist Theological Seminary, I referred the students to two excellent leadership books: *Spiritual Leadership: Principles of Excellence for Every Believer* by J. Oswald Sanders and *Spiritual Leadership: Moving People On to God's Agenda* by Henry and Richard Blackaby. In a chapter on "The Leader's Role: What Leaders Do," the Blackabys propose five elements of the spiritual leader's task:[6]

1. The spiritual leader's task is to move people from where they are to where God wants them to be. God's purposes take precedence

---

6 Henry and Richard Blackaby, *Spiritual Leadership: Moving People on to God's Agenda* (Nashville: B&H, 2001), 20-24.

over personal agendas in ministry. The key to spiritual leadership is for spiritual leaders to understand God's will for them and their organizations, and move people to do it.

2. Spiritual leaders depend on the Holy Spirit. Only the Holy Spirit can accomplish spiritual change in people. Pastors in and of themselves cannot change people; the Holy Spirit must work within them to bring about spiritual change.

3. Spiritual leaders are accountable. Spiritual leadership necessitates an acute sense of accountability to God's will.

4. Spiritual leaders can influence all people, not just God's people. Although spiritual leaders will generally move God's people to achieve God's purposes, God can also use them to exert significant godly influence upon unbelievers.

5. Spiritual leaders work from God's agenda. God's concern is not to advance leaders' dreams and goals or to build their kingdoms. His purpose is to turn His people away from their self-centeredness and their sinful desires and to draw them into a relationship with Himself.

Another fine book on Christian leadership that I recommend is *The Character of Leadership: Nine Qualities that Define Great Leaders* by Jeff Iorg, president of Gateway Seminary. The nine qualities Iorg identifies are the following:[7]

1. Maintaining integrity. A pastor does not practice double-dealing, double standards or having double meanings in what he says. Integrity has an ethical dimension of righteousness, holiness, and purity. Integrity occurs when you integrate your beliefs and actions with the standards of Scripture so there is consistency in your life. Your beliefs and actions

---

7 Jeff Iorg, *The Character of Leadership: Nine Qualities that Define Great Leaders* (Nashville: B&H, 2007), 23-225.

conform to the lordship of Christ and what the Bible teaches. Striving for full integrity must become part of your DNA and that of your church or Christian organization. An old saying comes to mind: "Do what is right and leave the consequences to God; do what is wrong, and you shall be compelled to take care of the consequences yourself."

2. Finding security. Secure leaders feel less pressure to perform, less pressure to please people, and less pressure to prove their worth by their accomplishments. The greatest source of security is a saving relationship with Jesus Christ and abiding in Him (John 10:27-30). Ministers have had leadership failures for surrendering to the "dark side" of unmet needs and existential debts that orient our lives and drive us from deep down inside. Some examples of the dark side are pride, selfishness, self-deceit, and wrong motives. I remember reading once about a minister driven to build a large church to prove to his father that he was competent, having heard from his father growing up that he didn't have it together and would be a failure in life.

3. Maintaining purity. No failure is more devastating to ministry leaders, their followers, and their families than moral failure. Ministry leaders represent God and are therefore expected to be honorable in personal relationships. God trusts pastors and Christian leaders to be morally pure and represent a standard of moral purity in the world. Some pastors, sadly, have brought shame and reproach to the name of Christ, their churches, and families by immoral and illegal conduct. Remember, "Blessed are the pure in heart, for they shall see God" (Matt. 5:8).

4. Learning humility. Humility is appropriate self-appraisal, seeing yourself as God sees you, adopting God's perspective on who you are and what you are assigned to do. Humility is said to be the hallmark of the spiritual leader. John the Baptist understood it well when he said about himself in relation to Jesus, "He must increase, but I must decrease" (John 3:30).

5. Developing servanthood. Servant ministry and leadership is defined more by who you are than by what you do. It is so important to have proper motives in ministry as you wash feet like Jesus did. Pastors are bondservants of Jesus Christ. Paul wrote, "For do I now persuade men or God? Or do I seek to please men? For if I still pleased men, I would not be a bondservant of Christ" (Gal. 1:10).

6. Gaining wisdom. Pastors must learn to be wise from biblical principles and associations with wise and responsible Christians. Proverbs 13:20 speaks loudly: "He who walks with wise men will be wise." Wisdom is knowing God and applying that knowledge in moral and spiritual matters, in handling dilemmas, in negotiating complex relationships. Many times in pastoral ministry when I did not know what to do, James 1:5 came to my mind: "If any of you lacks wisdom, let him ask of God, who gives to all liberally and without reproach, and it will be given him."

7. Practicing discipline. This is the self-discipline required in walking with Christ, controlling your emotions, and maintaining good habits. Before we can conquer the world, we must conquer the self. Discipline makes sacrifices to gain adequate preparation for what God has called pastors to do. When I think of spiritual self-discipline in ministry, the words of 1 Corinthians 9:27 ring loudly: "But I discipline my body and bring it into subjection, lest, when I have preached to others, I myself should become disqualified."

8. Showing courage. If there is anything pastors need in carrying out the work of the Lord, it is courage — facing our fears in the power of Christ with truth, appropriating God's presence and power. Prayer and steps of faith help us to have courage in leading God's people. Leaders need courage of the highest order when dealing with moral and physical issues in ministry, as well as dangers and difficulties. Have you memorized this verse? "I can do all things through Christ who strengthens me" (Phil. 4:13).

9. Sustaining passion. Passion is compassion displayed for the glory of God as you connect with people. Changing how you see people is vital for sustaining passion in ministry. Colossians 3:23: "And whatever you do, do it heartily (enthusiastically, with all your heart) as to the Lord and not to men, knowing that from the Lord you will receive the reward of the inheritance: for you serve the Lord Christ (Col. 3:23-24).

Two other essential qualities of leadership not mentioned in Iorg's book are these:

Casting vision — The ability to see more and farther than others and convey that to individuals who are following their leader. This is an attribute of faith. The great missionary pioneers were men and women of vision. I well remember a chapel message at Southwestern Baptist Theological Seminary by Jerry Falwell, who shared how the Lord would speak to him in his early morning quiet time to "Write the vision and make it plain on tablets that he may run well who reads it" (Hab. 2:2). Falwell began Thomas Road Baptist Church with thirty-five members that grew to a megachurch, a national syndicated radio and television ministry known as The Old Time Gospel Hour, a Christian academy, Liberty University, the Moral Majority, and numerous other ministries impacting the lives of people for good.

Making decisions — Clear, Christ-centered decisions are the mark of a true leader. A visionary may see, but a leader must decide. A pastoral leader must weigh evidence and make decisions on sound biblical premises and principles. Our decisions will reflect our values. Your best decisions will certainly be bathed in prayer and reflection upon scriptural principles.

Billy Graham on Leadership

Pastoral leadership is a course in and of itself. It has been said that "leadership is forged in the furnace."[8] I once heard or read early in ministry that great men are prepared for great deeds by great trials. Pastors have a learning curve, and there will be intense heat in pastoral ministry. President Truman's remark is certainly apropos here: "If you can't stand the heat, get out of the kitchen."

Billy Graham's evangelistic organization was very careful about four areas of ministry as committed to in the 1948 Modesto Manifesto, and pastors in their leadership roles must constantly be on guard for four enemies: **(1) mishandling finances** (be strict about how the Lord's money is handled); **(2) sexual immorality** (avoid being alone with women); **(3) criticisms of fellow ministers** (especially on minor points of doctrine, practices, or even failures in ministry); **(4) exaggerated accomplishments** (always tell the truth in reporting information. Credibility is a precious commodity; without it, people will not follow your leadership. When a leader exaggerates in one area, followers wonder if they are getting the unvarnished truth in other areas).[9]

Why Christian Leaders Make Mistakes

Some years ago, I came across a list (source unknown) of why Christian leaders make mistakes (errors in judgment) in ministry. Let me be honest and say that I fell victim to some of these myself in early years in pastoral ministry.

- Human, fallible judgments of the flesh
- Lack of correct information/facts

---

8 Harold Myra and Marshall Shelley, *The Leadership Secrets of Billy Graham* (Grand Rapids: Zondervan, 2005), 18.
9 "The Modesto Manifesto," accessed 21 July 2021, https://billygrahamlibrary.org/on-this-date-the-modesto-manifesto.

- Haste — too big a hurry to launch the plan or project
- People not ready for change — timing issue
- Pride; wanting to look good at all costs
- Erroneous assumptions
- Personality conflicts
- Trusted people who didn't follow through or prove reliable
- Faith lacking; didn't have enough faith in the Lord
- Lack of consultation with the Lord
- Inattention to details
- Not consulting with others
- Presumptions without facts
- Didn't talk to people that the decision affects
- Lack of experience (a bank of knowledge)
- Change for the sake of change
- Too sensitive to criticism
- Unwilling to make a decision — procrastination
- No clear direction

Church Administration

Church administration accompanies pastoral leadership, but administration has different functions from those required by leadership. Administration is one of the gifts of the Holy Spirit to the church. The Greek word *kubérnesis* translated as "administration" is used in 1 Corinthians 12:28. This gift is certainly necessary in God's work in order that all things may be done decently and in order in a church or Christian organization (1 Cor. 14:40).

The following are general concepts and principles utilized in effective and efficient administration that may be applied in churches. Some of these principles I learned in seminary in a course in church administration taught by Dr. Dennis Williams, professor of Educational Ministries and

Administration, Denver Seminary (1971-94) and dean of the School of Christian Education, Southern Baptist Theological Seminary (1994-2005):

— **Planning.** This general concept emphasizes the need to forecast or predict the future of an organization and to develop a program accordingly. A most crucial aspect of the entire planning process is that of policy making, a subject that will become increasingly important to the administrator as the organization enlarges. Planning is the process of examining the past and the present in order to construct the best program for achieving the organization's objectives in both the present and future. The ever-present need, of course, is to forecast as accurately as possible the circumstances that will exist in the future and then plan the program in the light of such knowledge. This requires the collection and the interpretation of relevant data from past programs (both successful and unsuccessful), and also from present ones, so that judgments of a dependable nature can be made for future action.

Planning, therefore, studies the past and the present, gathers data, interprets it, and then develops plans with the ultimate end in mind of achieving the organization's established goals. Jesus understood this concept when He said, "For which of you, intending to build a tower, does not sit down first and count the cost, whether he has enough to finish it — lest, after he has laid the foundation, and is not able to finish, all who see it begin to mock him, saying 'This man began to build and was not able to finish.' Or what king, going to make war against another king, does not sit down first and consider whether he is able with ten thousand to meet him who comes against him with twenty thousand? Or else, while the other is still a great way off, he sends a delegation and asks conditions of peace" (Luke 14:28-32). It is significant to note that budget preparation in churches and Christian organizations is very important in planning.

— **Organizing.** How does one go about structuring the church organization and arranging people so that they are suitably related to each other, so that they understand to whom they are responsible, and from whom they may receive assistance? An important role of a pastor doing church administration is to organize the functions and tasks necessary to accomplish the church's mission and ministry.

Organizing is occupied primarily with the proper arrangement of processes and individuals with their concomitant authorities and responsibilities (as often seen in organizational charts) within an institution. Jesus understood the importance of organization, when, in the feeding of the five thousand, He instructed the apostles to make the people all sit down in groups on the green grass in ranks, in hundreds and in fifties (Mark 6:39-40). Organization, therefore, is concerned with setting up an effective and efficient operation to accomplish the mission and tasks of the church.

— **Delegating.** One of the most important administrative activities of any organization is that of assigning specific duties to others. No leader, no administrator, can do everything. He or she must learn to delegate some of the work to other persons and then permit them to carry out their duties without interference in so far as the assigned work is performed satisfactorily.

The importance of delegation is clearly seen in Exodus 18:13-24 when Jethro advised Moses to delegate many of his duties to others. Jesus made assignments to the disciples when He sent them out on missions to preach, teach, and heal.

— **Staffing.** Perhaps the most difficult administrative task today in churches and organizations is that of getting the right persons in the proper positions of responsibility. Jesus spent a night in prayer before selecting twelve disciples to bear witness to His life and to carry on His work on earth after He returned to His Father in heaven (Luke 6:12-16).

Recruiting, training, and retention of high-quality personnel are key functions of administration. Writing good job descriptions is also important in staffing, as well as setting up a useful system of evaluating personnel. The military uses a system of Management by Objectives, where objectives are agreed upon by the supervisor and the individual, and the progress toward accomplishment is reviewed periodically.

— **Implementing or Executing.** The execution function requires strong intentional leadership to get the mission and goals of the church accomplished. This is a significant aspect of the administrative function in which you see to it that the work gets done. It is your opportunity to be effective, producing the decided, decisive, and desired effect. Effectiveness is said to be getting the right things done — and efficiency is getting things done right. You take the initial steps to put the plan into action. This is the executive function, and many decisions will be made in carrying out the mission and operational planning of the church.

— **Coordinating.** It is one thing to arrange the personnel in an organization effectively, but it is an entirely different matter to coordinate their activities so that they are efficient — productive without waste — in the respective operations. Coordination is the means whereby much confusion and duplication of effort are materially reduced. And it is also the means whereby many conflicts, tension, and resentments are eliminated through the integration of activities.

Coordination is the act of achieving unity and harmony of effort in the achievement of organizational goals. It is, in other words, the regulation of activities so that efficiency of operation results. It is getting people in the church to work together harmoniously to achieve the mission of the church with minimum expenditure of effort and material. Coordination is concerned with efficient operation of plans within the church so that objectives are easily attained. Communication and cooperation are thus essential elements of effective coordination. Jesus undoubtedly spent time in coordinating the activities of the disciples.

— **Supervising and Controlling.** One of the final steps in the administrative process is the determination of the organization's progress toward its stated goals and objectives. Experience has shown that it is not enough to plan, organize, delegate, staff, implement, and coordinate when there is no systematic means for checking on each aspect of the operations.

Projects may have been assigned and duties delegated, but are they being carried out, and to what extent? Checking with key personnel in a program on a continuous basis is the only method for avoiding persistent absenteeism and program failures. Church staff members and volunteer leaders must be supervised responsibly and lovingly. Good supervisors establish timelines and deadlines for projects and assignments to be completed. This is supervision. Oftentimes in churches with volunteers, this aspect of administration does not take place very well.

Jesus made it a point to meet with His disciples, following up their ministry assignments for reports (Mark 6:30; Luke 9:10). This supervision function sees to it that plans are carried out properly. Control consists in making sure that everything is carried out in accordance with the plan that has been adopted, the organization that has been set up, and the directions that have been given.

Control is a strong word for churches, but it is basically the means of seeing to it that the work flows smoothly and systematically through the organization consistent with plans. As a pastor, you will need to have a handle on budgets, budgetary review, analysis, and control. A chief accounting officer of a business enterprise or institution is often called a comptroller or a controller; in churches, this person is usually a treasurer — or, in larger churches, an executive pastor. The use of "in-process reviews" (IPRs) can be an integral aspect of the controlling function of administration. The "where are we at?" reports from staff members and volunteer leaders are key components in controlling.

— **Evaluating.** The last step in good administration is the evaluation and assessment process, like a football coach meeting with assistant coaches and players to review what went right and what went wrong on the field at the game. When I played football in high school, the coach often had "skull sessions" on Monday afternoons with the whole team when we looked at video clips and talked about good and bad plays on Friday night.

This last function is often the most neglected task of good administration. Evaluation seeks to "conserve the results" of the leadership and administrative process. Good administrators must seek to benefit from the previous strategies, programs, and operations to apply those "lessons learned" the next time. The military is well known for using "after action reviews" and "after action reports." Evaluation is the function to appraise the process and the product of the organization. In churches, we need to do a much better job at evaluating our programs, projects, and ministries.

Literature on Church Administration

Some good books on church administration are the following:

- Robert K. Bower, *Administering Church Education: Principles of Administration for Ministers and Christian Leaders*. Grand Rapids: Eerdmans, 1964.
- Aubrey Malphurs, *Advanced Strategic Planning: A New Model for Church and Ministry Leaders, 2nd Edition*, Grand Rapids: Baker, 2005. This book covers how to do an analysis and evaluation of the church by a strategic planning committee that looks at the core values of the church, develops a mission statement, creates a vision, and enacts a ministry strategy in which a strategic plan is formulated, funded, implemented, and evaluated.
- Bruce P. Powers, ed., *Church Administration Handbook*.

Nashville: B&H, 2008.

- Robert H. Welch, *Church Administration: Creating Efficiency for Effective Ministry, 2nd Edition*. Nashville: B&H, 2011.

Church Finances

An area many pastors feel least prepared to lead their church in is stewardship in general and church finances. The size of the church doesn't matter, as most churches expect and depend upon their pastor not only to raise the finances but to ensure that the finances are managed in a God-honoring way after they are collected. I usually did a good job in raising the funds and am thankful to have had treasurers and finance committees who did a fine job with the budget in the churches I served as pastor.

Church finances are important because the church's mission in the world is to make disciples, and it takes funds to do that. As a part of discipleship, the pastor must hold the congregation accountable for the stewardship of God's resources in the same way he would hold the church accountable for any of the other biblical admonitions regarding evangelism and discipleship.

It has been said that there are more than 2,300 verses in the Bible that address the topic of money. The Bible warns the people of God against storing up treasure on earth, for where our treasure is, there our heart will be also (Matt. 6:19-21).

Through the years, I have read and heard reports across denominational lines that 20 percent of the people in a church typically give 80 percent of the money. I always attempted to be proactive to get the church members to give the first fruits (tithe) of all their increase (Prov. 3:9-10; Mal. 3:1-12; Matt. 23:23), and for the members to spend wisely what is given to God on the mission and ministry of the church.

Church finances begin with the church having a strategic budget for how the funds will be spent. Responsible church members with their finances in good order need to be on the finance committee to develop a budget for presentation to the church at large in a congregational business meeting. Some financial experts advocate zero-based budgeting for organizations. In zero-based budgeting, every year those constructing the budget start over, and the previous year's allocations have no bearing on future allocations. This eliminates expenditures that have become routine over the years that no one challenges, even though they should be.

Some pastors have been called to serve churches with large indebtedness, which can be a great burden for them and the churches. I have known of pastors who have launched successful giving campaigns to pay off church debt; others have negotiated with banks and mortgage companies to reduce the size of the payments in view of extending the time to pay off the loan.

Churches, from time to time, will find it necessary to plan additions to facilities, buy property, or construct new buildings. Generally, to pay for such projects, the church may have funds set aside in savings, or there may be a major donor who has committed to providing a large gift. Sometimes a capital campaign will need to be launched. Pastors and building committees will need wise guidance before getting into a major building program. The final cost will almost always be much more than originally budgeted for with changes and cost overruns.

Before accepting the call to a church, pastors normally will be offered an income with benefits that typically include salary, housing allowance, mileage (travel) for church business, professional expenses (books and materials), expenses for annual associational and denominational meetings, medical insurance, and retirement. Churches usually review the salary of the pastor and church staff each year as part of the budgetary process. In the churches I served as pastor, I never asked for a raise in salary or benefits; I trusted the Lord to guide the finance committee to adequately compensate in view of increases in the cost of living.

Churches need a volunteer or paid financial secretary to record the tithes and offerings of the church members and send an annual statement of what has been given during the year for IRS purposes. Individuals who give cash need to put it in envelopes and write their name and the amount on the outside of the envelope.

Literature on Church Finances

The most comprehensive book I can recommend on church finances is *Money Matters in Church: A Practical Guide for Leader*s, Grand Rapids: Baker, 2007, written by Aubrey Malphurs and Steve Stroope. An author of more than twenty books on church life, Malphurs is a former professor of pastoral ministry at Dallas Theological Seminary and president of the Malphurs Group, a church consulting organization. Stroope is former senior pastor of Lake Pointe Church, Rockwall, which grew from 57 members to more than 15,000 in multiple campuses.

CHAPTER 13

TEAM MINISTRY AND DISCIPLESHIP TRAINING

As a pastor, you likely will have a church staff, volunteer or paid, to serve the Lord with you. Team ministry will be so relevant to a high-quality pastorate. Jesus had twelve ministry associates throughout His years of preaching, teaching, healing — and they had to be trained. He told His disciples on one occasion, "Take my yoke upon you and learn from Me" (Matt. 11:29). Elsewhere, He said, "For I have given you an example, that you should do as I have done to you" (John 13:15). The Apostle Paul wrote, "Therefore I urge you, imitate me" (1 Cor. 4:16) and "Imitate me, just as I imitate Christ" (1 Cor. 11:1). We were required to memorize 2 Timothy 2:2 in seminary, in which Paul wrote Timothy, "And the things that you have heard from me among many witnesses, commit these to faithful men who will be able to teach others also." Pastors must set a godly example for associates in ministry on the church staff.

Christ's method of training the disciples began with praying for guidance about which individuals He would choose to serve with Him (Luke 6:12-16). He carefully selected His ministry team from the many individuals who heard Him speak and followed Him. Those He called had to be willing to take up their cross daily (Luke 9:23). And Jesus spent quality time with those He was training to serve Him. Mark 3:14 notes that Jesus "appointed twelve, that they might be with Him." Their preparation for ministry was on-the-job training. He spent numerous hours with them in Capernaum and traveling, teaching as they walked and taught, and in different locations throughout Palestine.

A church ministry team will need guidance in view of the church's mission and ministry program. S. Lance Quinn writes, "Any effective pastoral ministry will emphasize spending valuable, Christ-honoring time with those who will eventually follow their pastor by entering the ministry ... If a pastor is going to reproduce himself in the lives of others, it will result from a purposeful association of spiritual fellowship and biblical nurturing."[1] There is a deep joy in mentoring and supervising individuals in ministry as we have been taught and mentored.

Over the years, as a pastor and Army chaplain, church and chapel staff meetings were special times each week to discuss prayerfully the work of the Lord. Our goal was to honor Christ in all that we planned to do, remembering how Jesus wanted the disciples and those who would believe in Him through their ministry to be as spiritually united as He and the Father were one (John 17:18-23). Paul wrote the church at Ephesus, "Endeavoring to keep the unity of the Spirit in the bond of peace" (Eph. 4:3). Nothing is more discouraging in ministry than disharmony among church staff and members of the congregation.

Church Staff Ministry

As a pastor (or senior pastor), you may have a church staff — whether it is a paid staff of full-time or part-time associates, or individuals serving

---

1 S. Lance Quinn, "Discipling" in *Pastoral Ministry: How to Shepherd Biblically*, John MacArthur and The Master's Seminary Faculty (Nashville: Nelson Reference & Electronic, 2005), 268-269.

in a volunteer capacity. As a church grows exponentially, it will not be possible for the pastor to minister personally to the entire congregation. I would think more than 250-300 active members would necessitate a paid associate minister. Some churches have paid part-time music, youth, children, senior adult, and outreach ministers.

Significant church growth will mean that the senior pastor cannot return every phone call immediately, grant every request for an appointment and counseling, contact every visitor, or visit each member who goes to the hospital or rehab, particularly if the church has many senior adults. If the church has lay elders and deacons, the pastor has some resources to assist him with pastoral ministry if there is no church staff. In fact, one of the best things a pastor can do in ministry is to train a group of "lay shepherds" to assist him with pastoral care.

John Bisagno writes, "There is no greater blessing and no greater need than a smoothly functioning, well-trained, hardworking staff of loyal, godly men and women assisting their pastor in the work of the ministry. Aaron held high the hands of Moses, and deacons freed the apostles to priority to the ministry of the word and prayer."[2]

If you are called to a church and inherit a church staff, you will have to prayerfully work with the staff members the best you can. If you have the privilege of selecting new staff members, you will certainly want to seek godly, qualified, well-trained, and experienced associates to assist you in ministry. Sometimes the best person you can invite to your staff is a close friend in ministry whom you know well and trust.

The pastor (senior pastor, lead pastor) is the chief elder of the church; he leads and supervises the church staff. The following are some key points to remember when you have a church staff.[3]

---

2 John Bisagno, *Pastor's Handbook* (Nashville: B&H, 2011), 329.
3 Ibid., 330.

1. Loyalty to the pastor is expected. Working behind the scenes against the pastor has no place on a church staff. If a staff member cannot support the pastor, he or she should resign and move on before being removed for disloyalty.

2. Developing good relationships with the staff must be a priority; unity within the staff is a must. If the pastor and staff are not united, it will flow downhill to the rest of the church. Jesus, remember, called His disciples "friends" (John 15:15).

3. Staff members should be given freedom to be productive and creative. However, the buck stops with the pastor. New ideas should be discussed and approved by the pastor before they are enacted.

4. Accountability is not negotiable; the pastor is accountable to the church for the actions of the church and the staff members. Pastors at times will have to correct staff members or overrule their decisions. When you do, don't talk about the staff member behind his or her back to another person. Always seek reconciliation when relationships have been damaged in the work of the Lord.

5. Treat staff members the way you would like to be treated. Remember the words of Jesus: "Therefore, whatever you want men to do to you, do also to them ..." (Matt. 7:12). Luke put it this way: "And just as you want men to do to you, you also do to them likewise" (Luke 6:31). The Golden Rule certainly needs to be practiced in staff relations. Friendship is essential in staff ministry.

The pastor will have to ask associates to make visits, counsel, and preach for him. When I was a single adult minister in a large church in Denver, the staff took turns a week at a time to make hospital visits. Staff meetings are needed for coordination of the church's ministry and programs. Ask the staff to come prepared with reports and recommendations for the meeting so that the meeting will not have to go on for hours. Begin the meeting with Scripture reading, devotional thoughts, and prayer.

Staff retreats away from the church office are good every six months or so each year when the mission, vision, and projects of the church are reviewed and evaluated, the calendar considered, and new ideas for ministry are explored. Spiritual brainstorming is one way to find creative ministries.

Ministry Teams

Ministry teams are essential to success in churches or church-related organizations. One of the best examples of a successful ministry team that stayed together to the end of their lives was the Billy Graham Evangelistic Association Team, made up of enormously gifted men who had been on promising career paths of their own, but they subordinated themselves to the group ministry to which each of them had been called.

A godly team will embody biblical principles of ministry, the formation of teams under the leading of God's Spirit for mutual encouragement, accountability, and discernment. Team players in Christian ministry know that the greatest success is the entire team's victory.

It is important to have the right people on the team. A corporate leader is known to have said, "I'd rather interview fifty people and not hire anyone than hire the wrong person." How true that will be in Christian ministry teams. Leaders have spoken on the importance of chemistry on a ministry team that blends personality, temperaments, spiritual gifts, and abilities to build a great team based upon loyalty, trust, respect, and *esprit de corps* based on shared goals. The wrong chemistry can blow up the best-laid plans and programs. The leader must have confidence in the team.

Working harmoniously together in the church and in organizations is an essential factor in effectiveness. I have said this before: Effectiveness is doing the right things; efficiency is doing things right. I was always glad when there were individuals on the team who were very competent in what they did. I concentrated on effective ministry to people and programs that were designed to impact lives, leaving the efficiencies to the staff. Mother Teresa knew about harmonious team ministry when she said, "You can do what I cannot do. I can do what you cannot do. Together we can do great things."

Cliff Barrows, longtime music and program director for the Billy Graham Evangelistic Association, once described Billy Graham's relationship to the team this way: "He was confident in God ... He sought God's will, he was God-dependent, motivated by his love for God and man. He was self-effacing, but he was secure in the place of God's appointment. He was anointed of God. He was considerate. He was not authoritarian. He knew that in the multitude of counselors there is safety. His decisions were based on mutual agreement rather than on a dictatorial basis. He thought about and relied on the counsel of those he trusted. He never was demeaning nor reprimanding. He trusted people and respected their contribution."[4]

In the Army when I served as a chaplain, the chaplain and the chaplain assistant were called the Unit Ministry Team (UMT). The chaplain did most of the spiritual ministry to include the preaching, teaching, counseling, visiting the sick and afflicted, memorializing those who had been killed or who had died, and attending the commander's meetings. The chaplain assistant is trained in warfare and carried the weapons to defend the chaplain (a non-combatant since WWI) in combat, drive the vehicles, and perform all of the administrative duties to include typing the bulletin and letters, setting up for worship services, prayer breakfasts, programs, supervising the counting and depositing of the collections, and anything the chaplain needed help with.

---

4 Harold Myra and Marshall Shelley, "Forming the Team" in *The Leadership Secrets of Billy Graham* (Grand Rapids: Zondervan, 2005), 51.

Qualities Needed in Building a Ministry Team

In seeking individuals to serve on a ministry team, the following qualities will be important:

Servant spirit — has a servant's heart and wants to help.

Character — has inward qualities that honor God and reflect Jesus Christ.

Godliness — moral and spiritual integrity based on God's Word in their life.

Submission — does not mind being supervised by leaders.

Passion — enthusiastic and excited about ministry to people and the program of the church.

Giftedness — endowed by the Holy Spirit with unique talents and abilities useful in ministry in the church and world evangelism and discipleship.

The following would be important in building an effective ministry team (source unknown):
- Look for individuals passionate about ministry.
- Recruit to a purpose, not a position.
- Provide adequate training.
- Value the generalist as well as the specialist.
- Avoid overworking volunteers.
- Have clear job descriptions and expectations.
- Develop the right foundation based on trust.
- Develop a trusting environment.
- Develop an empowering environment.
- Develop an encouraging environment.
- Develop a supportive environment.
- Develop accountability.

How Billy Graham and His Team Avoided Scandal in Ministry

For the sake of emphasis, I have repeated the Four Key Components out of the "Modesto Manifesto" adopted by Graham and his ministry team in 1948:

1. **Honesty** — report the truth about size of crowds and the number of inquirers.
2. **Integrity** — open book on how money was spent and publish a report of where and how monies were spent.
3. **Purity** — avoid temptation and compromising situations — never being alone with a woman, remaining accountable to one another.
4. **Humility** — never speak badly of another Christian minister, much less another Christian.[5]

Characteristics of Effective Ministry Teams

If your congregation relies on leadership teams to make ministry happen, the vitality of your church depends on these groups working well together. Strong ministry teams, generally display the following characteristics, adapted from an article by Ann A. Michel:[6]

1. Shared vision. A good team understands what it needs to accomplish and how its work connects to the overall vision of the church. Ministry teams give it their all when they feel something real is at stake. Strong teams coalesce around significant challenges.

2. Distinct roles. A team functions most effectively when every member has a unique and vital role to play. On a baseball team, for

---

5 Myra and Shelley, *The Leadership Secrets of Billy Graham*, 53-58.
6 "5 Characteristics of Effective Ministry Teams" by Ann A. Michel, Lewis Center for Church Leadership, 29 July 2015; accessed 2 July 2021; https://www.churchleadership.com/leading-ideas/five-characteristics-of-effective-ministry-teams).

example, the pitcher and the catcher do different jobs, but neither can do their job without the other. Motivation, buy-in, and accountability are enhanced when each team member knows the group's success depends on their efforts. When you launch a team, think carefully about what different roles are essential. In a group that has worked together for some time, pause occasionally to ask what needs to be done and who should be doing it.

3. Constructive engagement. Teams achieve good outcomes when they get all the relevant issues on the table and fully evaluate their options before making decisions. Team members thus must feel free to express their opinions honestly and even risk disagreeing with one another. This type of open and honest engagement only occurs in an atmosphere of trust and mutual respect. Strong teams are deliberate in building this type of decision-making climate. In the military, when staff members had to brief a commander with strategies representing different options, we prepared several courses of action with the pros and cons for each option to be discussed, weighed, and evaluated carefully; the commander would choose which course of action for implementation.

4. Size. Effective teams tend to remain lean. The group must be small enough for each person's participation to really matter. In larger groups, the style of communication often shifts from inquiry to advocacy, making it more likely that a few voices will dominate the conversation and less likely that all participants will engage openly.

5. Leadership. In strong ministry teams, every member provides leadership. But someone needs to take responsibility for making sure the team itself functions well. Good teams have a "captain" who maintains the focus on the vision, attends to the climate of the team, facilitates the group's processes, and keeps communication flowing.

CHAPTER 14

PASTORAL ETHICS, ETIQUETTE, POLITICS, LEGAL ISSUES, CHURCH DISCIPLINE

Pastors who are serving the Lord in ministry will be required to deal with moral, ethical, political, legal, and church disciplinary issues. Several stories come to mind about the thoughts and ways of Jesus in such situations. Early one morning in the Temple, some scribes and Pharisees brought a woman caught in adultery. They set her before Jesus and said, "Teacher, this woman was caught in adultery, in the very act. Now Moses, in the law, commanded us that such should be stoned. But what do you say?" (John 8:1-5).

These religious men were looking for something with which to accuse Jesus. Stooping down and writing on the ground with His finger, He raised up and said to them, "He who is without sin among you, let him throw a stone at her first" (John 8:7). One by one being convicted in their conscience, they went out from the oldest to the last man. Looking up, Jesus saw no one but Himself and the woman. He said to her, "Woman, where are those accusers of yours? Has no one condemned you?" She said, "No one, Lord." And Jesus said to her, "Neither do I condemn you; go and sin no more" (John 8:11).

As a pastor since 1971 and a military chaplain from 1980 to 2004, the most trying and troubling issues for me in ministry were dealing with moral and ethical issues of church members and military personnel. You will need the wisdom of God in such trials. That is why James wrote, "If any of you lacks wisdom, let him ask of God, who gives to all liberally and without reproach, and it will be given to him" (James 1:5).

Dealing with political and legal issues is another challenge you will have as a pastor. The pastor of my home church in North Carolina when I was a boy dealt with alcoholic beverages being sold in the county (my county was a dry county). Pastors have dealt politically and legally with such issues as racism and segregation, the removal of prayer and Bible reading from public education, abortion, pornography, homosexual marriage, euthanasia, the national debt, involvement in wars, and other issues being discussed and voted on in the nation.

Politically, another situation in the life of Jesus comes to mind when the Pharisees and Herodians attempted to entangle Him in His talk by asking Him, "Is it lawful to pay taxes to Caesar or not?" (Matt. 22:17). Jesus perceived their wickedness and said, "Why do you test Me, you hypocrites? Show Me the tax money." So they brought Him a denarius, and He said to them, "Whose image and inscription is this?" They said, "Caesar's." And He said to them, "Render therefore to Caesar the things that are Caesar's, and to God the things that are God's" (Matt. 22:18-21). When they heard this, they were astonished at His teaching. In ministry situations, we need to "be wise as serpents and harmless as doves" (Matt. 10:16) regarding legal and political issues. Be prepared to represent the Lord from the teachings of Scripture. More will be said about legal issues in church and church discipline.

Pastoral Ethics

One of the old standard texts of another generation used in Christian pastoral ministry training is Nolan B. Harmon's *Ministerial*

Ethics and Etiquette, first copyrighted in 1928, then 1950 and 1978, with editorial revisions added in 1987 to make it more acceptable to women in ministry. If there was ever a day when ethics (morals) and etiquette (manners) in the lives of ministers need revival, it is certainly today, especially in the United States.

In the introduction, Harmon writes, "The Christian minister today, whether conducting some impressive rite of his church, or preaching the Word, or ministering to the poor, or perhaps helping his wife in some menial task about the home, has the opportunity at all times to *make honorable the calling* which God has placed him."[1] The Apostle Paul wrote Timothy, "Let the elders who rule well be counted worthy of double honor (respect and financial support), especially those who labor in the word and doctrine" (1 Tim. 5:17). Those who serve in the pastorate earn respect by a ministry of integrity that glorifies God.

The first chapter of Harmon's book offers a high view of ministry, reminding us that Christian ministry is esteemed the noblest of the professions. Ministry is indeed a high calling, not as a mark of personal honor to our self, but an honor to the One (Jesus Christ) who first called us. Harmon makes ten thought-provoking points about the conduct of Christian ministers in his book[2]:

1. The minister must keep the nobility of his calling uppermost in his own mind. Paul advises us not to compare ourselves with others but to seek God's glory and approval in our ministries (2 Cor. 10:12-18).

2. The minister must hold high in outward acts the established reputation of the Christian ministry. The community expects a closer adherence to moral standards on the part of the minister than from

---

1 Nolan B. Harmon, *Ministerial Ethics and Etiquette* (Nashville: Abingdon, 1987), 16.
2 Ibid., 17-30.

the ordinary man. Paul's advice is apropos here: "All things are lawful unto me, but all things are not expedient" (1 Cor. 6:12). We must not use our freedom in Christ to dishonor our Lord and be a bad example for others.

3. The minister must never forget that he is one who serves. The Apostle Paul understood this well when he wrote, "For I say, through the grace given to me, to everyone who is among you, not to think of himself more highly than he ought to think, but to think soberly, as God has dealt to each one a measure of faith" (Rom. 12:3).

4. The minister must never for reasons of personal safety desert his parish and people when some great, universal danger impends. Speaking of the good shepherd, Jesus said, "But a hireling, he who is not the shepherd, one who does not own the sheep, sees the wolf coming and leaves the sheep and flees; and the wolf catches the sheep and scatters them. The hireling flees because he is a hireling and does not care about the sheep" (John 10:12-13).

5. The minister must utilize his time properly. There is an appropriate time for everything (Eccl. 3:1-8) and pastors must make the most of time management for the sake of his family and church.

6. The minister must never measure his work by the salary involved. Harmon says it well: "The laborer is worthy of his hire and must have it; but with the Christian ministry it is the work and not the wages which must be supreme."[3]

7. The minister must guard the use of his name. "The pastor should not give sanction or endorsement to those causes or movements that are questionable."[4] Proverbs 22:1 says, "A good name is rather to be chosen than great riches."

8. A minister must not encroach upon the field of another

---

3 Harmon, *Ministerial Ethics and Etiquette*, 26.
4 Ibid., 28.

profession. A minister must not try to be something he is not — a psychiatrist, psychologist, physician, or lawyer. Endeavor to be a man of God who knows the Word of God and the God of the Word.

9. The minister must not lower his profession by becoming a "handyman" for all the members of his church. Yes, the minister will be the chief servant in serving the Lord and people, but he is not to be an errand boy for the community. Get other Christians to help you as the apostles did in Jerusalem when they asked the church to select seven men of good reputation, full of the Holy Spirit and wisdom, to handle the business of distributing the food in the Jerusalem church (Acts 6:2-4).

10. The minister must hold his professional service in such esteem that he will keep it from being dissipated in the maze of shallow channels of service that open out in all directions today. A minister has a higher calling than to promote all the noble causes in the community. Harmon says it so well: "The minister is called to preach the unsearchable riches of Christ Jesus, and anything less than this cometh of evil. Let the pastor avoid all sidetracks that lead off the main highway. Let him confine all his energies to his own great mission — and God will abundantly reward those efforts as one attempts to live out the high calling of Jesus Christ."[5]

Pastoral Etiquette

Here are some tips on etiquette I learned from pastors I served with in ministry:

Be careful not to be critical of other ministers of the Christian gospel. If you must critique something, critique what is being taught erroneously and practiced.

---

5 Harmon, *Ministerial Ethics and Etiquette*, 30.

Dress appropriately for the occasion in moderation. Don't try to draw attention to yourself in what you wear in the pulpit.

Watch your body odor. Use deodorant. You don't want to smell badly to your church members or prospects.

Watch your breath. Keep breath mints close at hand — especially at the time of public invitation, or for greeting people at the doors of the church, or when you speak to people in close proximity.

Have clean fingernails and shoes that are shined. You are not working in the yard or a field when you are doing church ministry inside the church, homes, assisted living apartments, hospitals, rehab centers, and nursing homes.

Send handwritten thank you notes for gifts, meals, and anything anyone does for you. Your thanks must go the second and third mile. People will appreciate you for it.

Use good manners at the table. Don't be proudly undignified and unrefined. Especially don't talk with your mouth full. During my first year in pastoral ministry, I bought a copy of Amy Vanderbilt's *Complete Book of Etiquette*.

Stand for people out of respect, especially women and older men coming to the pulpit or entering your office. Better to stand for all. Pull chairs out for women seated next to you; open and hold doors for women near you; better still, do these things for all people out of courtesy.

Have some business cards printed and keep a variety of care-giving cards. Take get well cards to people in the hospital, send cards in grief situations, and have some good evangelistic tracts and some encouragement cards for people who are going through crises. I like to send birthday and anniversary cards to members of the congregation with a personal note written.

The Pastor and Politics

In the early days of American history, pastors informed the electorate concerning the moral issues of the day. Today, secular media and adversarial courts would like to keep God's Word from influencing governmental laws and policies. Ever since the Ten Commandments, Bible reading, and prayer were removed from public education in the 1960s, America has been on a moral downslide.

Whose responsibility is it to educate the population on the issues relating to marriage, family, decency, and moral rightness? The media, the government, Planned Parenthood, American Civil Liberties Union, movie stars and famous athletes, academic think tanks and professors in secular colleges and universities think they should guide the politics of the nation. John Bisagno writes, "Preachers must once again accept the responsibility of informing the citizenry, but it will require exceptional moral courage" for the men of God to thunder forth, "Thus saith the Lord!"[6]

Today, there is a strong movement to make it illegal to speak against homosexuality, lesbianism, and transgenderism. The nation is moving toward enacting laws against speaking against these aberrant moral sins as "hate speech." It is important for the pastor to know what is legal and what is not legal when he addresses moral issues that are also political issues. Of course, in elections a pastor and church should not endorse candidates; however, a church can inform the congregation of what candidates believe on moral issues. It is probably not a good idea to have candidates speak from the pulpit at a church. If the pastor and church want to hear a candidate, it is best to do it somewhere other than church facilities.

What can pastors do in relation to the political issues of the day?

- Proclaim and explain the truth of God's Word, addressing moral

---

6 John Bisagno, *Pastor's Handbook* (Nashville: B&H, 2011), 445.

issues impacted in political decisions. Inform and educate God's people of what His Word teaches about moral and social issues.
- Encourage church members to register and vote in elections, using their votes to influence the nation for good.
- Assist the church to know what candidates believe by distributing voter guides that outline the policies and positions of individuals being considered for office.
- Encourage the church members to pray about running for public office and standing for righteousness in the community and nation. Proverbs 14:34: "Righteousness exalts a nation, but sin is a reproach to any people." Psalm 33:12: "Blessed is the nation whose God is the Lord, the people He has chosen as His own inheritance."
- Lead Christians in your church to pray for the nation and its leaders (2 Chron. 7:14 and 1 Tim. 2:1-2).

Should a pastor ever run for political office?

While this is not a normal course of action for pastors leading churches, it is possible that God might lead a gospel minister to run for a political office. Jesse Jackson, a minister, was a candidate for his party's nomination to run for president in 1984 and 1988; Pat Robertson, an ordained minister in Virginia, was a presidential candidate in his party in 1988; Mike Huckabee, a former pastor, became governor of Arkansas and campaigned for his party's presidential nomination in 2008 and 2016; Andrew Young, a pastor in Georgia, became mayor of Atlanta and later served in the House of Representatives for many years.

Legal Issues in Ministry

Pastors certainly need to be informed about the governmental laws that relate to churches, because churches are being sued these days and very often are losing the cases either through out-of-court settlements or judicial verdicts. This is a very litigious age in which we are living.

A pastor "must understand clearly that a church is generally responsible for everything that takes place in its buildings, on its premises, on rented equipment or property, and virtually everything under the influence or sponsorship of staff or other persons, whom the court would identify as 'an agent of the church.' This means the church is legally responsible not only for activities that occur on its property but would, for example include incidents that occur away from the church in a vehicle that had been rented to transport students to a youth retreat, as well as at the retreat itself."[7]

Churches must have insurance not only for fire and other catastrophic events but also liability insurance that will cover accidents and incidents in the church. I once played in a father-and-son basketball game at church on a Wednesday night and drove to the basket for a layup. A kid tried to block me, and I knocked him down. The next week he was in a wheelchair with a broken leg. I apologized to the father and offered to pay the medical expenses, but it had already been taken care of by the church's insurance. On a youth outing at a skating ring one Saturday night, I (the pastor) fell and broke my right arm badly, requiring two surgeries. This, too, was covered, thankfully, by the church's liability insurance. I have not been roller skating since. The church building and parsonage of the church I was serving as pastor of in 1989 during Hurricane Hugo had much damage from the storm, but it was all covered by insurance.

As a pastor, you will need to coordinate with your church leadership and staff to make sure your church is adequately protected against liability and other claims against the church through insurance. Some

---

7 Bisagno, *Pastor's Handbook*, 371.

common church liability issues are the following: personal injuries, property damage, premise liability, child abuse and neglect claims, negligent hiring or retention of staff members, sexual misconduct, defamation.

The church must take the greatest care to protect the church from lawsuits regarding negligence in protecting children and teens from abuse. State laws require the pastor to report every known incidence of child abuse. This is not protected by confidentiality or privileged communication. Confidentiality does not require pastors to report adult spousal abuse or even crimes committed by adults in the past. However, if an individual tells you about harm he or she intends to inflict upon another person, you tell them that confidentiality just ended with that disclosure.

John Bisagno says it so right when he writes, "Every pastor should lead his church in establishing policies and procedures that reduce the risk of child abuse occurring in the church. And the law requires you to report known and even alleged incidences of child abuse."[8] There is not a better article on protecting the church against child abuse than one written for publication by Cheryl Markland of the Baptist State Convention of North Carolina, offering sound advice about protecting children and teens in the context of church ministry.[9] In addition, here are some legal protections that pastors need to be informed about.

Articles of Incorporation

Churches in the United States should incorporate as a non-profit corporation under the laws of the state in which they are domiciled/located so that if there is legal proceeding against the church, the legal action is against the entity and not the individuals of the corporation.

---

8 Bisagno, *Pastor's Handbook,* 372.
9 Cheryl Markland, "Five Ways to Guard Against Child Abuse in Your Church," accessed July 5, 2021, https://ncbaptist.org/5-ways-to-guard-against-child-abuse-in-your-church.

In Texas, unincorporated churches are treated by the state as if they are incorporated when it comes to suits against the actions of the church through its officers and official representatives.

501(c)(3) Status

Churches may apply for 501(c)(3) status as a tax-exempt organization so that contributions are considered tax deductible. Tax exempt status does not excuse or exempt an organization from maintaining proper records and filing any required annual or special-purpose tax returns.

Organizations with 501(c)(3) status are prohibited from conducting political campaign activities to influence political elections for individuals campaigning for public office.

Ecclesiastical Abstention Doctrine

In effect, this doctrine maintains that as long as churches do not violate federal and state criminal and civil laws, the government does not interfere with the laws, rules, regulations, policies, and procedures of how churches are self-governed.

Church Discipline

No practice of the early church is more neglected in our day than church discipline. Church discipline has been regarded as one of the marks of a true church. Yet somehow we do not see ourselves in the church today as "believers joined together by the bond of the Spirit and associated by covenant in a shared confession of faith in the Lord Jesus Christ and a common fellowship of the gospel," according to R. Stanton Norman.[10] I think we see ourselves as autonomous and independent

---

10 R. Stanton Norman, *The Baptist Way: Distinctives of a Baptist Church* (Nashville: B&H, 2011), 64.

Christians who are free to serve God on our own terms without a sense of accountability to God through the local church in which we are a member.

Norman notes how the church has moved away from communal accountability toward autonomous individualism. He suggests that the general lack of respect for authority in society has impacted ministerial authority. Sadly, ministers have been involved in corrupt morality and practices and have brought upon the church a low view of pastoral authority. Another issue is how easy it is to transfer from one church to another without the church member's prior status at their previous church being investigated. Many churches do not accept letters of transfer from churches not of the same denomination. In other words, anyone who is disciplined or censured can consequently leave one denomination or local church and join another without any difficulty, particularly in large communities where members know nothing about an applicant for membership.

And the fact remains that many Christians do not want to be accountable to other Christians whom they don't really know or trust, so spiritual accountability is all but nonexistent in many Baptist and independent congregations. Norman raises the issue of the potential for loss of funds if a popular member or the leading giver of the church is disciplined. Another issue is the rising fear of litigation, or the church being sued for damaging a person's reputation.

Such legal action was not the case in Baptist churches in the past. This loose view of church membership probably began sometime after the turn of the twentieth century. Baptist churches before 1900 attempted to follow the teachings of Jesus and the apostles regarding the holiness and health of the church. Norman writes, "Baptists believed that our beliefs, mission, witness, proclamation, spirituality, governance, fellowship, and morality were tied to the faithful practice of discipline."[11]

Jesus Himself laid down guidance for church discipline in Matthew 18:15-20. The teaching of binding and loosing follows the disciplinary procedures laid out to deal with sinning brethren, in which Jesus says the authority of heaven will back up the church's decision to discipline and to liberate a repentant brother or sister. The holiness and righteousness of God in His people are at stake in the church's testimony before the world. This does not mean that the church is to be mean-spirited and hypocritical in its approach to church discipline, but it should be love-focused — and just as in disciplining our children, love must be tough and not permissive, lest we raise irresponsible and defiant children. Church discipline is an attempt to rescue an errant believer from destructive patterns of life that threaten the message and ministry of the church. Church discipline also keeps sin from spreading and contaminating the rest of the congregation.

Church discipline is important because God is holy and He has called the church to be holy and set apart unto Him, reflecting His holy character as revealed in Jesus Christ (1 Peter 1:15-16; Hebrews 12:7-11). Church discipline is a means by which God's holiness in the world is seen and preserved. The Hebrews passage reminds us that God Himself chastens or disciplines those He loves.

The writings of the Apostle Paul remind us that the early church practiced church discipline. We see this especially in 1 Corinthians 5:1-13 where an unrepentant man who was having sex with his father's wife was to be excommunicated, put out of the church, because such immorality defiles the character and testimony of the church of Jesus Christ. Paul knew that there would be repentant sinners formerly guilty of all kinds of sins in the church (1 Cor. 6:9-10) when he

---

11 Norman, *The Baptist Way,* 65.

wrote, "And such **were** some of you. But you **were** washed, but you **were** sanctified, but you **were** justified in the name of the Lord Jesus and by the Spirit of our God" (1 Cor. 6:11). The fact that they were once immoral and intemperate in their living, and were cleansed by the blood of Christ, means they were no longer living in sin. And to continue in sin after Christ has set you free is to bring reproach on the name of Christ and His church, not to mention judgment on yourself. Church discipline will not be necessary when Christians are spiritually disciplined by living in the way, the truth, and the life of Christ. Scripture, time and again, calls for discipline of the will: "Therefore do not let sin reign in your mortal body, that you should obey it in its lusts" (Rom. 6:12). Paul knew about spiritual discipline when he wrote, "For if you live according to the flesh you will die; but if by the Spirit you put to death the deeds of the body, you will live" (Rom. 8:13); "I am crucified with Christ" (Gal. 2:20). Paul admonished the church at Galatia to walk in the Spirit and they would not fulfill the lust of the flesh (Gal. 5:16) because those who are Christ's have crucified the flesh with its passions and desires (Gal. 5:24). Read Romans 6-8 where Paul teaches that the victorious Christian life can be a reality for every believer.

The process of disciplining the unrepentant man referred to in 1 Corinthians 5 appears to eventually have led to his repentance and restoration to the church, as 2 Corinthians 2:4-8 indicates that the apostle reminded the congregation to forgive and comfort the repentant man and to restore him back into the fellowship.

Other Scriptures remind us of the work of church discipline: Galatians 6:1 provides instruction for restoration and cautions against pride. The church at Thessalonica was to warn and eventually withdraw from those who had rejected the teaching of the apostles to the point that they had quit working and were sponging off the church (2 Thess. 3:6-15). Regarding false doctrine, the Apostle Paul wrote Timothy to excommunicate Hymenaeus and Alexander for blasphemy (1 Tim. 1:20). Elders or overseers who sinned were to be rebuked publicly as a warning to others (1 Tim. 5:19-20) because Christians, no matter how prominent or esteemed, are not above the discipline of the church. Titus was given instructions to withdraw from divisive people and their controversial and heretical speculations (Titus 3:9-11).

Church discipline is referred to by Anabaptists and Baptists in their early confessions of faith. For example, the First London Confession of the Particular Baptists (1644) states that every member is subject to congregational discipline and that the local church ought with great care and tenderness, with due advice, to proceed against her members. The document entitled *Charleston Church Discipline* (1774) defines three types or degrees of church censure: (1) the rebuke, admonition, or brotherly reproof; (2) suspension "from office, from the Lord's table"; and (3) excommunication, or exclusion from union and communion with the church, and from all rights and privileges thereof.

History reveals that church discipline was widely practiced by the majority of Baptist churches before the twentieth century. While the Scriptures do not lay out exactly what sins are to be disciplined, those sins that bring reproach on the name of Jesus and His church would be a beginning point, and would certainly include unresolved issues between church members (Matt. 18:15-17; 1 Cor. 5:5-6), false doctrine (1 Tim. 1:19-20; 2 Tim. 2:17-18; Rev. 2:14-16), divisiveness (Rom. 16:17-18), unrepentant sexual immorality (1 Cor. 5:1-11), and disorderly conduct (2 Thess. 3:6-15) as leading contenders. I would think also that if a church member is publicly conducting dishonest and fraudulent business practices that injure people, not only should the court be involved but also the church. These sinful practices were in the public domain and were known about by the church at large. Paul writes about Christians suing one another in courts when they should have been dealing with these issues in the context of the church (1 Cor. 6:1-8).

Regarding public wrongdoing, Norman writes, "The public nature and knowledge of the sins brought reproach on the church, impugned the integrity of its message and mission, and dishonored the cause of Christ. Further, the refusal of the church to address such matters would have signaled the approval of the congregation and could have encouraged others to follow the sinful practices that were publicly tolerated in the fellowship."[12]

The teaching of Jesus in Matthew 18:15-18 outlines four stages of church discipline:

(1) Step one (Matt. 18:15) — recognition of the offense and going in private to the offender to seek reconciliation. If the offender recognizes his sin and repents, the offended person should have a measure of satisfaction of reconciliation. If the offender will not admit wrongdoing and repent, and he is guilty, other members of the church are to be involved.

(2) Step two (Matt. 18:16) —Jesus here points to Deuteronomy 19:15 that says a person may not be convicted of a crime on the basis of a single witness. At least two witnesses are necessary to ensure that an accusation is made with integrity, truthfulness, and in an unprejudiced manner. The other individuals are necessary witnesses in the event the case must go to a higher level. They are also there to attempt to assist in the attempted restoration. If the second level with witnesses does not work, then another step is needed.

(3) Step three (Matt. 18:17a) — Here Jesus said, "Tell it to the church." There are pastors who believe this means the assembled congregation, while others select a representative group from the larger

---

12 Norman, *The Baptist Way,* 72. A Baptist student in training for the pastorate or a pastor would do well to buy a copy of *The Baptist Way: Distinctives of a Baptist Church* by R. Stanton Norman. His chapter on church discipline, 64-83, is a good review of this important practice often neglected in modern churches.

corporate body of the church to deal with these accusations.

Norman adds, "The public inclusion of the congregation in the process indicates that the church body is ultimately responsible for the discipline of its members."[13] Norman continues: "The church must discern the facts of the situation and render a judgment based on the teachings of the Word of God. The deportment of the church in this stage must always be Christlike, with the goal being the restoration of the sinning brother or sister."[14] If this does not work, Jesus offered a final piece of guidance.

(4) Step four (Matt. 18:17b) — If the individual does not pay attention even to the church, he is to become like an unbeliever and a tax collector to the church. The church is to treat the unrepentant individual as an unbeliever and withdraw fellowship or excommunicate the errant individual. When a person will not submit to the discipline of the church, then he or she is no longer considered a part of the church, just like individuals outside the church who do not see themselves accountable to Christ and His church. If the individual comes before the church and repents, the church must certainly forgive him, comfort him, and confirm their love to him (2 Cor. 2:6-8).

Church discipline is never something pastors look forward to. I personally think this issue should be handled by the pastor and a committee of committed church members before ever being brought before the gathered church.

Literature on Church Discipline
- Adams, Jay E. *Handbook of Church Discipline: A Right and Privilege of Every Church Member.* Grand Rapids: Zondervan, 1974.

---

13 Norman, *The Baptist Way,* 74.
14 Ibid.

- Garrett Jr., James Leo. *Baptist Church Discipline*. Paris, AR: The Baptist Standard Bearer, Inc., 2004. Originally published: Nashville: Broadman Press, 1962.
- Laney, J. Carl. *A Guide to Church Discipline*. Minneapolis, MN: Bethany House, 1985.
- Richardson, Wyman Lewis. *Walking Together: A Congregational Reflection on Biblical Church Discipline*. Leader's Guide and Student Workbook. Eugene, OR: Wipf & Stock, 2007.
- White, John and Ken Blue. *Church Discipline That Heals*. Downers Grove: InterVarsity Press, 1985.

Literature on Restoring Fallen Pastors
- Armstrong, John H. *Can Fallen Pastors Be Restored? The Church's Response to Sexual Misconduct*. Chicago: Moody Press, 1995.
- Grenz, Stanley J. and Roy D. Bell. *Betrayal of Trust: Confronting and Preventing Clergy Sexual Misconduct*, Second Edition. Grand Rapids: Baker Books, 1995, 2001.
- LaHaye, Tim. *If Ministers Fall, Can They Be Restored?* Grand Rapids: Pyranee Books, Zondervan, 1990.
- Narramore, Clyde M. *Why a Christian Leader May Fall*. Westchester, IL: Crossway Books, 1988.
- Wilson, Earl and Sandy, Paul and Virginia Friesen, Larry and Nancy Paulson. *Restoring the Fallen: A Team Approach to Caring, Confronting & Reconciling*. Downers Grove: InterVarsity Press, 1997.

CHAPTER 15

BLOOM WHERE YOU ARE PLANTED

Pastors are called by God and a church to serve in spiritual leadership. The Lord may keep you in one location for your entire career of ministry, or you may be led to move to different ministry assignments. I never envisioned serving the Lord as a pastor, military chaplain, and college/seminary/university professor of ministry in different locations when I declared my calling to vocational ministry to my home church in 1970. In my earliest years in ministry, Billy Graham's ministry made such an impression on me that I wanted to be an evangelist like him, but the Lord opened doors for me to do evangelism as a pastor and chaplain.

In the Parable of the Talents, Jesus told these words to the man given five talents and the one given two talents that doubled what had been entrusted to them: "Well done, good and faithful servant: you were faithful over a few things. I will make you ruler over many things. Enter into the joy of your lord" (Matt. 25:21, 23). In speaking about faithfulness in what belongs to another, Jesus said, "He who is faithful in what is least is faithful also in much; and he who is unjust in what is least is unjust also in much" (Luke 16:10). This principle certainly applies to the way in which pastors lead and serve God's people in churches. Faithfulness in a ministry may lead to increased responsibility in another ministry in the will of God.

A pastor is not an evangelist, traveling teacher, or church planter like the apostles and their associates, remembering how Jesus sent the Twelve and the Seventy on preaching missions. While Capernaum seems to have been His headquarters, He Himself traveled throughout Palestine in His preaching, teaching, and healing ministry. Circumstances often required Him and the apostles and disciples to move on when their message was not accepted, and the fires of persecution prevailed. In such cases, Jesus told them to "depart from that house or city, shake off the dust from your feet" (Matt. 10:14).

In addition to his evangelistic, missionary, and church-planting travels with the Apostle Paul, Timothy (born ca. AD 17) eventually served as a pastor in Ephesus. Paul's two letters to Timothy give considerable guidance about church leadership and ministry. Tradition has it that he served as the first bishop of Ephesus until AD 97, when he was clubbed to death by a mob for protesting the orgiastic worship of the goddess Artemis.

Let me encourage you to be faithful to the ministry to which God has called you. You don't need a prestigious position in a church to be faithful to the gift and calling you have received from the Lord. Paul makes this point to Timothy when he says, "Let no one look down on your youthfulness, but rather in speech, conduct, love, faith and purity, show yourself an example of those who believe. Until I come, give attention to the public reading of Scripture, to exhortation and teaching. Do not neglect the spiritual gift within you" (1 Tim. 4:12-14).

Rich Gregory of Grace Community Church writes, "Be faithful with what God has put before you today. When God providentially places a task in front of you, be faithful to it as unto Him, no matter how menial that duty may seem. In order to *become* a man of God, you must first *be* a man of God. Seminary is not a salvific experience where you are changed and made into something that you once were not. Either you are a pastor or you're not. Additional training is not suddenly going to make you into a faithful servant. Faithfulness to your calling must be who you are today."[1] If you are faithful in the assignments the Lord will give you, you may be very surprised where your ministry will take you.

In the eighteenth and nineteenth centuries, it was not uncommon for pastors to serve one church for their entire ministerial career. However, this is normally not the case today. The average tenure of Baptist pastors during the past several decades from statistics I have seen has been several years. Typically, the largest and strongest churches have had pastors who stayed in the pastoral office at the church for a long time. However, from time to time the Lord calls pastors to move to other churches and into teaching ministries at colleges, universities, and seminaries. Some pastors are called to chaplaincy ministry or denominational leadership. This, of course, is not leaving the ministry but receiving a different assignment from the Lord.

What It Means to Bloom Where You Are Planted

Young pastors have a tendency to be thinking about the next church they want to serve while they are involved in their present ministry. This reminds me of the old saying in higher education teaching and administration that speaks of "working the chairs." Not only is ambition for success in ministry a challenge, but pastors can get discouraged when everything doesn't go as planned and they are often ready to look for another church to serve.

The pastorate is not easy, as there will be opposition, criticism, misunderstanding, and conflict in the daily work of ministry. Jesus knew this would be the case when He sent out His disciples and told them, "Behold, I send you out as sheep in the midst of wolves. Therefore,

---

1 Rich Gregory, "Stewardship and the Call to Ministry," accessed 7 July 2021, https://blog.tms.edu/stewardship-and-the-call-to-ministry.

be wise as serpents and harmless as doves" (Matt. 10:16). You have divine resources from the Lord to help you — the wisdom of the Word of God, the power of the Holy Spirit, your prayer time, and seasoned pastors and godly Christians you can talk with for counsel and support.

John Bisagno understood the pastor's desire to succeed in ministry: "I fear the secular world has placed an unreasonable pressure on young pastors to succeed. Success is not measured by numbers. The size of your congregation and percentage of growth, so important to the world and far too often to our peers, is not the measure of success in the eyes of the Father. Integrity. Holiness. Commitment. Faithfulness. These are qualities dear to the heart of God in the lives of His servants."[2] And self-promotion is not the way of the Lord, so don't ask people to recommend you to certain churches and don't recommend yourself. Jeremiah the prophet wrote some great advice one day: "And seekest thou great things for thyself? Seek them not" (Jer. 45:5).

God's shepherds are often looking for greener pastures when they ought to be praying and working more diligently to make the pasture they are serving in a place of great blessedness for Christ's sheep. I once read a good piece of advice that if you want to pastor a large church, build a big fire where you are serving, and others will see the smoke and come and try to lure you away. The largest churches in America began as small churches and they grew by the devoted and diligent work of the pastor and people. A good piece of advice is to "bloom where you are planted" by preaching and teaching the Word faithfully, sharing Christ with the lost, discipling the new converts, and giving high-quality, compassionate pastoral care to church members.

We must be very careful that we don't put limitations on where the Lord may want us to serve. I must admit I wanted to serve the Lord

---

2 John Bisagno, *Pastor's Handbook* (Nashville: B&H, 2011), 86.

as a pastor either in California (where my wife is from) or in North Carolina (my home state). The closest I got to California was pastoring in Colorado, and the closest I got to pastoral ministry in North Carolina was Virginia and South Carolina. I always wanted to pastor a large church, but the Lord directed me to serve smaller churches and chapel ministries with less than 250 members and attendees. My larger ministries were as a chaplain in the Army.

In the kingdom of God, it is more important for us to be in the place of the Lord's appointment than to try to make our youthful dreams of ministry success come true. That does not mean that we should not have a vision, goals, and dreams for reaching people and ministering to them with every fiber of our being.

The Pastor Changing Churches
Unfortunately, there are times when a pastor will experience conflict within the congregation he is serving, which may lead to him being asked to resign — or he will start looking for another church, and may even resign because he feels he is not able to resolve the conflict. There may be other reasons for a pastor to move or resign — for example, the need for an increased salary if he has children going to college. Some pastors have experienced burnout, discouragement, or even clinical depression over their ministries and have resigned from pastorates.

A rule of thumb to consider is "stay where you are if you can." While the grass may look greener on the other side of the fence, there are advantages to staying where you are placed by the Lord. As one pastor said it, "At least I know what the problems are in my church. I don't know what they are in another church."

A pastor certainly needs to renew himself and his ministry from time to time to keep from getting into a pastoral rut. Pastoral conferences, seminars, and continuing education are resources pastors can tap into to improve their ministry skills and have their spirits encouraged. I have been blessed through the years by conferences for pastors in my denomination and at the Billy Graham Training Center at The Cove, Asheville, North Carolina.

The bottom line for changing churches is the will of God. Charles Spurgeon, in Great Britain, offered some advice about this once with an illustration of three lighthouses — saying that when a captain was able to line up the three lighthouses, one directly behind the others, it was safe to enter the harbor. James Bryant and Mac Brunson explain the three lighthouses in a pastor's life that should line up in determining the will of God[3]:

— First, there is **the lighthouse of the Word of God**. A pastor must believe in consulting the Scriptures about whether it is God's will for him to accept another church; otherwise, it is best for him to turn down the offer.

— Second, there is **the lighthouse of circumstances**. God does guide through circumstances — and the pastor must carefully consider the circumstances of the possible change, especially in relation to his family situation. The strength of the call may also be a consideration. Church bylaws typically stipulate a certain percentage of favorable votes for the call, often 90 percent or better. I have heard of pastors unwilling to accept a call unless it is a unanimous vote. Some churches after the initial vote count, will then ask for a unanimous vote.

— Third, there is **the lighthouse of the inner witness of God's Spirit**. God's Spirit leads and guides those who are willing to follow. If you do not have this inner spiritual leading, you better stay where you are.

---

3 James W. Bryant and Mac Brunson, *The New Guidebook for Pastors* (Nashville: B&H, 2007), 209-11.

When It Is Time to Move

The proper time to leave a ministry is an issue for which there are no easy and absolute answers. Pastors should certainly consult the Lord via Scripture for principles, praying for the guidance of the Holy Spirit, and seeking counsel from godly Christians for wise counsel. While teaching pastoral theology, ministry, and leadership at Southwestern Baptist Theological Seminary, students asked me to develop a biblically based lecture with principles on "When It is Time to Move," and the following is what the Lord gave me from reflective thought in Scripture. Let me encourage you to read and reflect upon the Scriptures referred to.

Have you completed the work God gave you to do in a certain place for a certain length of time? (John 4:34, 17:4; Acts 20:24; 2 Tim. 4:7). God's work is never completely finished, but what He has called you to do in a certain place will eventually come to an end. Even Jesus, in His prayer to His Heavenly Father before the disciples, prayed, "I have finished the work which You have given Me to do" (John 17:4).

Has a new open door of ministry been presented to you? (1 Cor. 16:9; 2 Cor. 2:12-13; Rev. 3:8). **Has the Holy Spirit closed one door and opened another for ministry?** (Acts 16:6-10). Just because there may be an open door, that does not mean that there will be smooth sailing, as was the case with the early apostles and followers of Jesus.

Have you been rejected and persecuted for your gospel preaching, teaching, and ministry and you believe you should move on to another harvest field? Adversity and conflict may require that you move from your present place of ministry to another (Matt. 10:14; Luke 10:10-11; Acts 8:1). This was certainly the case of Jesus and the early apostles.

Are you growing spiritually, and are the people growing with you? Have you been wholeheartedly loyal to Christ, living a godly life, and yet the people of the church are not following your spiritual leadership? If so, you may be casting your pearls before swine; the people may not be responsive to your spiritual life, leadership, and ministry (Matt. 7:6). This may be a reason to move.

Is your family being adequately taken care of? (1 Cor. 9:4-14; 1 Tim. 5:8, 18). You have a responsibility to provide for your family. I made several moves for this reason, having a goal for as much Christian schooling and higher education as possible for our children. They have been blessed in their lives, ministries, and vocations for the commitment my wife and I made to their Christian education.

Have you fasted, prayed, and sought a word from the Lord through the work of the Holy Spirit about this with other Christian church leaders? (Acts 13:1-4). God will often use fellow ministers who are in tune with God to be a source of guidance and direction. I would not have become an Army National Guard chaplain in addition to pastoring and serving as an administrator and teacher at a Christian college were it not for a retired Air Force chaplain and an Army National Guard chaplain who kept encouraging me to pray about an opportunity to expand my ministry to part-time military chaplaincy, which eventually led to full-time military chaplaincy.

Has God given you a vision for a new harvest field? (John 4:35-38). God gives those who lead His work visions for ministry and extending the ministry of the gospel of Christ.

Are your motives pure in your desire to move to a new field of ministry? (Jer. 48:10; Phil. 1:12-19; 1 Thess. 2:1-8). It is possible to serve in ministry with wrong motives, so it is important to keep check on your soul.

Are you using your spiritual giftedness where you are presently serving? (Rom. 12:4-8; 1 Cor. 12:1-11; 1 Pet. 4:10-11). Individuals not using all their spiritual gifts in ministry may feel a leading to move where they believe they can use their gifts.

Have you talked with wise, older, mature ministers about your desire to change ministries? (Prov. 13:20, 19:20). There is wisdom available in talking with seasoned, godly pastors.

Is there something you don't want to do or some place you do not want to go in ministry? Remember Jonah's call to go to Nineveh (Jonah 1:1-2) and how he tried to avoid it (Jonah 1:3-2:10). Are you open to be obedient to God? True faith and obedience go together like hand in glove.

CHAPTER 16

REVIEWING THE BASICS OF A PASTOR SERVING CHRIST IN A NEW TESTAMENT CHURCH

As we close out this last chapter, a wonderful passage to reflect upon regarding pastoral theology and ministry practices is John 15:1-8, a portion of the Upper Room Discourse Jesus shared with the apostles on the night before His crucifixion. Pastoral theology, leadership, and ministry are all about representing Jesus Christ in our beliefs, character, and ways of relating to people in and outside of the church. There's not a better passage to remind us of this.

In this allegory of the vine and the branches, Jesus reminded the apostles that He is the true vine, and His Heavenly Father is the vinedresser (gardener). The true vine is not Israel. The true vine is Jesus, the Word made flesh and dwelt among men (John 1:1, 14). The apostles beheld His glorious life full of grace and truth. As we represent Christ in life and ministry, loving grace and spiritual truth must be reflected and reproduced through us. The Apostle Paul wrote about Jesus Christ being the foundation for ministry, and our work in ministry will be tested by fire (1 Cor. 3:5-17).

God is compared to the gardener who will perform two roles: cutting off the branches that are fruitless and pruning those branches bearing fruit that they may bear more fruit, and more abundant fruit.

As God's Word is at work in pastors doing ministry, we are cleansed by the power of the Word of God through the Holy Spirit. Very likely Judas was in mind, who once was in fellowship with Jesus the vine but removed himself by betraying Him (John 13:18-30).

To bear spiritual fruit in ministry, we must abide in Christ. He must be ruling and reigning in our lives as we represent Him to the lost and the saved. Jesus said, "Without Me, you can do nothing" (15:5). A living union with Christ is absolutely necessary to produce spiritual fruit; without it, we are nothing. Not abiding in Christ is a danger in the Christian life and ministry because it can lead to withering and the judgment of God when spiritually barren branches will be cut off and burned. The imagery of fiery destruction is, of course, figurative, but it serves as a warning against apostasy, turning away from Christ and betraying Him as Judas did.

I cannot forget hearing my seminary president, Vernon Grounds, in a chapel worship service admonish us students preparing for ministry to "Remember Chuck Templeton." Templeton, born in 1915, was a leading evangelist in America, a contemporary of Billy Graham, from 1936-1959, preaching in stadiums in the 1940s and 1950s with crowds of up to 30,000 people and many professions of faith in Christ. Tragically, he became an agnostic and then embraced atheism after struggling with doubts. In 1996, he wrote *Farewell to God: My Reasons for Rejecting the Christian Faith*. Lee Strobel, a former atheist himself and author of *The Case for Christ*, interviewed Templeton three years before His death and Templeton confessed to Strobel that he adored Jesus and missed Him. His wife reported he had a deathbed experience when he saw angels and believed they were coming for him. Hopefully he turned back to the Lord at the end of his life.

On the other hand, when believers called to ministry abide in Christ and allow His Word to dwell in us, we will ask what we desire in ministry and God will be glorified by our lives and there will be answers to our prayers (John 14:12-14, 16:23-24). People will be saved and transformed by the power of Christ through our fruit-bearing ministries. This closing chapter will review eight basic responsibilities of the pastor serving a church.

Leader in Worship

While a number of church members and visiting Christians may be involved in worship services, the pastor as God's shepherd for the congregation is the leader in worship. As the "overseer to shepherd the church of God" (Acts 20:28), the pastor gives spiritual leadership, guidance, and direction to all aspects of worship services. This calls for prayerful planning with God in private in the study and with ministry associates in staff meetings. Music directors and music ministers today are often referred to as worship leaders in contemporary churches, a modern term seeking to be more relevant to younger people. However, the actual worship leader of the church is the pastor.

The early church gathered primarily to worship Jesus Christ as Lord. Typical of New Testament gatherings for worship was the house church, especially in Pauline congregations. The households in that day consisted of a network of people that included (in addition to the extended family) slaves, servants, hired workers, and others who may have been in the same trade group — as in the case of Lydia's household, which may have included women who were also "sellers of purple" (Acts 16:11-15). House church ministries are mentioned in some of Paul's letters: Romans 16:5; 1 Corinthians 16:19; Colossians 4:15; Philemon 1:2. Some of these smaller house churches were surely part of a larger Christian community in the large cities.

The house churches often grew out of the synagogues where Jewish believers in Christ became unwelcome at the synagogue — a natural model for Christian assemblies to follow, using the Septuagint (Greek version of the Old Testament) for Scripture reading as well as the literature produced by the apostles (Matthew, John, Paul) and assistants to the apostles (Mark, Luke, James, Jude). In addition to Scripture reading and a message, there would have been prayers, collections of the tithes, the singing of Psalms, hymns, spiritual songs, baptism of new believers, and the Lord's Supper — all under the oversight of the pastor.

Model of the Christian Life

The pastor knew, after being baptized into Christ's death and resurrection, that as a Christian he was expected to "walk in newness of life" (Rom. 6:4) and be holy as the One who called Him is holy (1 Pet. 1:15), having met the qualifications of 1 Timothy 3:1-7 and Titus 1:5-9 to be "blameless" with "a good testimony among those who are outside *the church*." His life was to reflect the Christ whom he followed and served. He was to walk in faith and obedience, teaching baptized believers to observe all things commanded by Jesus (Matt. 28:20). Throughout early Christian literature like *The Didache*, there are repeated descriptions of Christian morality contrasted with that of the pagan world. Roman entertainment in the arenas with gladiatorial battles, the circus, theater, and amphitheater had corrupt themes that were to be avoided. And pastors gave considerable time and energy to promoting the discipline of holy and righteous living within the congregation.

To be holy means to be set apart or separate from sin and evil because "God is light and in Him there is no darkness at all" (1 John 1:5). The Apostle Paul wrote Timothy, who became a pastor: "The Lord knows those who are His, and let everyone who names the name of Christ depart from iniquity" (2 Tim. 2:19). Pastors, like all Christians, were to have the mind of Christ in how they were to see people and understand situations in life: "Let this mind be in you which was also in Christ Jesus" (Phil. 2:5); "For who has known the mind of the Lord that he may instruct Him? But we have the mind of Christ" (1 Cor. 2:16).

The key to living holy as a model of the Christ-life is to love God (Matt. 22:37; Mark 12:30; Luke 10:27), love one another (John 13:34-35), and love one's neighbor (Matt. 22:39; Mark 12:31; Luke 10:27; Rom. 13:8-10 — a love that fulfills God's law.

Preacher of the Word

The pastor has an authoritative calling and role to fill in preaching the Word of God. Paul wrote Timothy, "I charge you therefore before God and the Lord Jesus Christ, who will judge the living and the dead at His appearing and His kingdom: Preach the word! Be ready in season and out of season. Convince, rebuke, exhort with all longsuffering and teaching, for the time will come when they will not endure sound doctrine, but according to their own desires, because they have itching ears, they will heap up for themselves teachers; and they will turn their ears away from the truth, and be turned aside to fables" (2 Tim. 4:1-4). The Word is biblical truth from the Scriptures, instructive exposition. Thus, it was expositional, exegetical, and prophetic.

It has been well said, "Every season of reformation and every hour of spiritual awakening has been ushered in by a recovery of biblical preaching."[1] As the pulpit goes, so follows the church. It was the recovery of expository preaching by the preachers of the Protestant Reformation of the sixteenth century that turned the church back to the faith of apostolic Christianity. The revival preachers in America in the eighteenth and nineteenth centuries brought spiritual renewal in churches and conversions of many people through the powerful preaching of the Word of God. Their messages called hearers to repent and believe the gospel.

---

1 Steven Lawson, "Preach the Word" (2 Dec. 2020), accessed 15 July 2021, https://www.ligonier.org/blog/preach-word.

Biblical preaching, especially expository preaching, will transform lives. Sadly, much of the preaching in churches today is laced with entertainment, video clips of current events, and shallow messages designed to attract non-church-going people. Sermons from the pulpit today are often filled with pop psychology and contemporary happenings in the culture designed to prick the ears of the hearers. People consequently get spiritual pablum rather than the strong meat of the Word of God.

The prophet Amos, in his vision of summer fruit, wrote, "Behold, the days are coming, says the Lord God, that I will send a famine on the land, not a famine of bread, nor a thirst for water, but of hearing the words of the Lord" (Amos 8:11). May we who are called to preach God's Word never contribute to a famine of the Word of God in our generation.

When Jesus went into the synagogue in Nazareth and was invited to speak, He turned in the scroll to Isaiah 61:1-2 and read from it, declaring, "Today this Scripture has been fulfilled in your hearing" (Luke 4:21). He obviously spoke from the text, as the people "marveled at the gracious words which proceeded out of His mouth" (Luke 4:22). The Apostle Peter preached a powerful message at Pentecost (Acts 2:14-39) in which he cited several Old Testament Scriptures and admonished the hearers to "repent, and … be baptized in the name of Jesus Christ for the remission of sins" (Acts 2:38). New Testament-era preachers believed they were delivering a message in harmony with God's will, based upon God's Word, out of which they had done exegesis with an application of the text to the lives of those who heard the Word. The sermon in the early church "was the primary medium for doctrinal instruction, as well as offering exhortation, encouragement, rebuke, praise, and consolation."[2]

---

2 Carl A. Volz, *Pastoral Life and Practice in the Early Church* (Minneapolis: Augsburg Fortress, 1990), 110.

Teacher of the Church

One of the qualifications for the position of bishop (overseer) is that he must be "able to teach" (1 Tim. 3:2; 2 Tim. 2:24 and Tit. 1:9), "holding fast the faithful word as he has been taught, that he may be able, by sound doctrine, both to exhort and convict those who contradict." The pastor must have an appointment by God as a teacher (1 Cor. 12:28). Teaching is a grace gift of God (Rom. 12:7) through Christ (Eph. 4:11) "for the equipping of the saints for the work of ministry, for the edifying of the body of Christ" (Eph. 4:12).

Before He ascended, Jesus instructed the apostles to make disciples by teaching them to observe all things He commanded them (Matt. 28:19-20). The apostles and the pastors who followed them were to have a powerful teaching ministry in the church. In the first centuries of the church, disciples were often instructed in the teachings of Christ for up to three years. Thus, the bishop/pastor became the primary teacher of the congregation. The Apostles' and Nicene creeds formed the basis of catechetical instruction. Biblical materials comprised these creeds and became both the content and source of instruction. Early Christian teachers often used stories and examples to illustrate biblical truth.

The Scriptures were the primary source for biblical instruction. The Apostle Paul wrote Timothy that "all Scripture is given by inspiration of God [God-breathed] and is profitable for doctrine [teaching], for reproof, for correction, for instruction in righteousness, that the man of God may be complete, thoroughly equipped for every good work" (2 Tim. 2:16-17).

Among priorities for the local church today, none is more important than teaching — and the pastor-teacher's responsibility is to instruct the church in the Christian life in view of eternal life. During His earthly ministry, Jesus was the master teacher. In His post-resurrection appearance to two men walking on the Emmaus Road, He expounded the Scriptures to them, beginning with Moses and all the prophets regarding the things concerning Himself (Luke 24:27). If Jesus prioritized teaching from God's Word, we who pastor His churches must do likewise and instruct people in the things of God.

Prayer Warrior

While a church must have people who pray for the ministry of the congregation, the pastor must take the lead by being a disciplined man of prayer, remembering how Jesus slipped away from the disciples for times of prayer with His Heavenly Father. A pastor's ministry will not rise any higher and be any deeper than his prayer life. A fellow brother in Christ once told me that prayer is the key to heaven, and faith unlocks the door.

There are many ways to pray like a warrior preparing for battle. The pastor's prayer life must begin early in the morning, and it will continue throughout the day and evening as a pastor interacts with his family, staff and church members/prospects in meetings, visitation, and counseling. Conducting mid-week intercessory times of prayer, special called prayer meetings, and occasional prayer retreats will impact and empower the life and ministry of the church. Pastors would do well to return to a time of pastoral prayer in the worship services of the church.

Before revival and evangelistic meetings in churches I served as pastor, I organized cottage prayer meetings to begin praying for the meetings and individuals who would benefit spiritually from attending the services.

Pastoral Care Giver

Care of souls is a responsibility pastors have been assigned by the Lord to lead out in the spiritual and physical welfare of Christians in the churches they serve. Pastors must devote time to the well-being of individuals during their various physical, emotional, and spiritual crises. Pastors must visit, counsel, and be available to church members when their lives are interrupted by unexpected trials of faith and spiritual, physical, and emotional maladies from within and without. Pastors and associates will visit individuals when they are in the hospital, rehabilitation centers, nursing homes, and assisted living, as well as in homes.Some personal crises will be the result of sin; others will be from situations not the fault of the individual. The best care that can be given by the pastor is the compassionate love of Christ in response to the teachings of Scripture: "Through love serve one another" (Gal. 5:13). Guidance from the Scriptures will provide the pastor a source of wisdom in one-on-one counseling. Church members will consult the pastor on most any troubling issue in their life. Empathic concern and care are needed by parishioners with troubled hearts and lives. Often, church members will approach the pastor about marital issues in a day when many people, including professing Christians, seek divorces for their unresolved marriage problems. Then there are deaths in the church when the pastor must provide care for bereaved parishioners and their families. Unfortunately, there will be the challenge of adjudicating disputes among church members, as was the case in Corinth when some of the believers were taking other believers to secular courts before unbelievers over issues between them, when they should have resolved the conflicts through the church (1 Cor. 6:1-8).

Church Leader and Administrator

A pastor is not only an elder (Acts 14:23; Tit. 1:5) but an overseer (Acts 20:28; Phil. 1:1; 1 Tim. 3:1-2; 1 Pet. 5:2), which implies he is an administrator of the work of Christ's church. As an under-shepherd of Christ to His people (John 21:15-17; 1 Pet. 5:2-4), the pastor must oversee the mission and ministry of Christ through the church. Secular overseers served in the Hellenic world and were attached to institutions as administrators "of burial associations, athletic clubs, and other special interest groups, including municipal governments. The office was simply one of overseer or general manager."[3] The church obviously took this term from the culture and began to use it in the congregations.

The gift of administration is a spiritual gift of Christ to the church (1 Cor. 12:28). The Greek term used is *kybérnēsis,* meaning a steersman or helmsman for a ship, with the responsibility of guiding the ship into the harbor through the rocks and shoals in all kinds of weather and situations. This pilot was an expert in the midst of a storm. Administrators, thus, are leaders who lead, guide, organize, and govern. They take charge and begin giving guidance and delegating responsibility when no one is in charge. Their style may differ, as was the case of the early apostles and spiritual leaders of the church. Pastors are administrators with the Spirit-given capacity and ability to serve God and His people by organizing, administering, promoting, and executing the affairs and ministries of a church.

Pastors are administrators with the Spirit-endowed capacity and ability to serve God and His people by organizing, administering, promoting, executing, and evaluating the affairs and ministries of a church. Your administrative skills will be needed in coordinating church planning and staff meetings with associates in ministry, elders, deacons, and committees, as well as supervising the budget of the church.

Promoter of Evangelism

The Apostle Paul wrote Timothy, "But you be watchful in all things, endure afflictions, do the work of an evangelist, fulfill your ministry" (2 Tim. 4:5). While the Lord gave some to be evangelists (Eph. 4:11), pastors

---

3 Volz, *Pastoral Life and Practice in the Early Church,* 16-17.

are not exempt from doing evangelism. Evangelism is proclaiming the gospel of Jesus Christ to others. Dwight L. Moody, Billy Sunday, Billy Graham, and Oral Roberts were popular preachers in America with dynamic evangelistic ministries.

However, local churches have benefited with church growth when their pastors actively promoted evangelism. Lee Roberson, R.G. Lee, W.A. Criswell, Jerry Falwell, Adrian Rogers, John Bisagno, John Osteen, Rick Warren, Ed Young, Tony Evans, and Andy Stanley have been effective pastors with the gift of evangelism. Many individuals came to Christ during their pastoral ministries featuring evangelistic altar calls, organized evangelistic visitation, and weeks of revival meetings.

Thom Rainer, former president and chief executive officer of Lifeway Christian Resources, asked pastors of evangelistic churches what they did to lead their churches to be more explicitly evangelistic. The nine most common responses are the following:

— **Pray that the church will become more evangelistic.** Conversion is an act of the Holy Spirit. Thus, these pastors depend on God to reach people before they introduce any type of human methodology.

— **Pray for opportunities to share the gospel.** I heard amazing stories from pastors about how God put people in their paths almost every time they prayed for such an opportunity. One pastor stated simply: "God does not give me a lack of opportunities if I ask Him to bring lost people my way."

— **Become accountable to someone else for sharing the gospel.** That person could be a family member, another church member, or another pastor.

— **Start new groups.** Churches that intentionally start new groups tend to be more evangelistic. These new groups could be Sunday school classes, small groups, or new ministries.

— **Preach the gospel.** While every sermon does not have to an evangelistic sermon in the classic sense, every message should point to Jesus. There should be some presentation of the gospel in all of the pastor's messages.

— **Celebrate new believers.** What is rewarded becomes normative. When pastors intentionally lead their churches to celebrate a person becoming a Christian, evangelism becomes a part of the DNA of church life.

— **Get the gospel in all the ministries.** Many churches have many dynamic ministries. Pastors should ask if every ministry is designed to point a person to Jesus.

— **Evangelize young people in the church.** Pastors of evangelistic churches seek to make certain that the youth in the church are presented the gospel. If churches were to evangelize "their own," the number of conversions would double or triple in most congregations.

— **Have a meal with a non-believer.** I borrowed this insight from Tony Merida. He encourages his church members to invite non-believers to have a meal with them on a regular basis. He makes a powerful case to demonstrate how often that was done in the New Testament.[4]

Dispenser of Benevolence

The Twelve who followed Jesus carried a moneybag (also translated money box) with funds for their own needs and distribution to the poor (John 12:6; 13:29). In the early church, tithes of food items and funds were brought to the bishop for distribution to the needy and downtrodden, as was the case in the Jerusalem church — a responsibility handled by the apostles until seven Spirit-filled men were selected by the church for this ministry (Acts 6:1-6). Deacons typically handled sharing what was

---

4 Thom S. Rainer, "9 Ways a Pastor Can Lead Their Church to Be More Evangelistic," accessed May 16, https://research.lifeway.com/2015/11/24/9-ways-a-pastor-can-lead-his-church-to-be-more-evangelistic.

given for those in need. Jesus had taught the disciples the eternal value of representing Him in providing food for the hungry, drink for the thirsty, shelter for the homeless, clothing for those without, as well as visiting the sick and those in prison (Matt. 25:31-46).

The Apostle John never forgot what He learned from Jesus about the outworking of love by giving when he wrote, "But whoever has this world's goods, and sees his brother in need, and shuts up his heart from him, how does the love of God abide in him?" (1 John 3:17). The Apostle Paul wrote Timothy to instruct the rich not to trust in uncertain riches but to do good by being ready to give, willing to share, storing up for themselves a good foundation for the time to come, that they may lay hold on eternal life (1 Tim. 6:17-19). Paul himself, in fact, organized a fund-raising effort among the churches he planted to collect funds for the poor Christians in Jerusalem (Acts 24:17; Gal. 2:10; Rom. 15:25-26; 1 Cor. 16:1-4; 2 Cor. 8:16-9:15).

As a pastor, you will have the opportunity to organize and promote support for the poor and needy in your church and community. Churches I served as pastor had closets for food and clothing distribution, and we provided hotel accommodations, food, and gasoline for travelers needing assistance. At times, we paid utility bills when poor people could not pay for heat and electricity. Sometimes it is wise for churches in a community to work together to take care of needy people.

Adjudicating Disputes

A pastor will assist church members in resolving conflicts in their personal life and with others. For the last eighteen years, I have taught, from time to time, a course in resolving conflict in ministry in a seminary and at a Christian university. One of my students on a large church staff told me recently that it was the most valuable course he took in seminary, as he spends considerable time helping individuals resolve their conflicts.

Christians will have serious differences of opinion in the work of the Lord. We see that in the case of the Apostle Paul and Barnabas as they prepared for a second missionary journey. Barnabas was determined to take with them John Mark, but Paul insisted that they should not take him with them since he had departed from them in Pamphylia and had not gone with them to the work. Their contention over this issue became so sharp that they parted from one another. The result was that Barnabas took Mark and sailed to Cyprus, while Paul chose Silas to accompany him to Tarsus, across Galatia, Phrygia, Mysia to Philippi, Thessalonica, Athens, Corinth, Ephesus, and back to Antioch (Acts 15:36-41).

Church Discipline Leader

One of the tasks of the pastor is to handle church discipline and the proceedings that may evolve from it (Heb. 13:17; 1 Pet. 5:1-4). Jesus taught the apostles steps to be taken in a church regarding a sinning brother (Matt. 18:15-17). Howard Sugden and Warren Wiersbe point out that "Matthew 18 describes the necessary ingredients for successful discipline: humility (1-6), honesty (15-17), obedience to the Word (18-19), prayer (20), and a forgiving spirit (21-35). Unless a church has the right spiritual atmosphere, attempts at discipline will do more harm than good. Before you can even begin to start practicing it, you must get the church into the right spiritual condition, and this takes time, prayer, love, and faithful teaching."[5]

Offenses serious enough to require discipline would certainly be the

---

5 Howard F. Sugden and Warren W. Wiersbe, *Answers to Pastors' FAQs* (Colorado Springs: Nexgen, 2005), 147.

following: (1) personal differences between two or more members; (2) refusal to earn a living; (3) doctrinal error; (4) repeated troublemaking; and (5) open sin.[6] Churches in their bylaws or adopted guidance typically have procedures stipulated for dealing with church discipline issues. The pastor should take the first step privately and see the offender, later involving other church leaders if necessary. I am thankful that the churches I served as pastor never had to publicly remove a believer from the church, as was the case of the unrepentant man in Corinth (1 Cor. 5:1-13).

Sugden and Wiersbe recommend that pastors and churches keep discipline matters from becoming public scandals particularly in regard to church officers: "There will be some cases when the wisest move is for the offender to resign quietly after making things right. If the confession is sincere, the officer will not balk at this suggestion. In situations involving theft, immorality, or defiance of authority, it's best for the offender to resign the office. The pastor will want to assist them with regular counsel."[7]

---

6 Sugden and Wiersbe, *Answers to Pastors' FAQs*, 148-49.
7 Ibid., 146.

About the Author

Richard Thomas Vann Jr. is director of the Master of Arts in Christian Ministry-Chaplaincy degree program at Dallas Baptist University. Originally from North Carolina, he is a graduate of Chowan University and Mars Hill University, with master's degrees from Denver Seminary, Wayne State University, US Army War College, and Southwestern Baptist Theological Seminary.

From 1969 to 1975, he served in the US Air Force and US Air Force Reserve. From 1980 to 2004, he served as a chaplain in the Colorado Army National Guard, US Army, and US Army Reserve, retiring from the Army with the rank of Colonel in 2004. He completed a PhD in foundations of education from the University of South Carolina in 2000 and a DMin in pastoral theology from Midwestern Baptist Theological Seminary in 2017.

Through the years, he has served civilian churches and military congregations as a pastor. In 2004, he was invited to join the faculty of Southwestern Baptist Theological Seminary as associate professor of pastoral ministry. In 2010, he joined the faculty of the Dallas Baptist University Graduate School of Ministry, where he teaches Christian ministry, chaplaincy, pastoral theology, spiritual formation and worship, Baptist heritage and polity, and New Testament classes.

Married to Marta Atwell from California, they have six married children and eighteen grandchildren. His wife, five of their children, four of the children's spouses, and a step-grandson are Dallas Baptist University graduates. Dr. and Mrs. Vann are members of First Baptist Church of Lakeside, and he serves an interdenominational Christian fellowship in a senior adult apartment complex in North Richland Hills.

www.ingramcontent.com/pod-product-compliance
Lightning Source LLC
Chambersburg PA
CBHW061257110426
42742CB00012BA/1949